Responsive Web Design for Libraries

ALA TechSource purchases fund advocacy, awareness, and accreditation programs for library professionals worldwide.

lita

Responsive Web Design for Libraries

A LITA Guide

Matthew Reidsma

ALA TechSource
An imprint of the American Library Association

CHICAGO 2014

Matthew Reidsma is web services librarian at Grand Valley State University, in Allendale, Michigan. He is the cofounder and editor in chief of *Weave: Journal of Library User Experience,* a peer-reviewed, open-access journal for library user experience professionals. He speaks frequently about library websites, user experience, and responsive design around the world. *Library Journal* named him a "Mover and Shaker" in 2013, which led to many unfortunate dance-related jokes in the Reidsma household. He writes about libraries and technology at www.matthewreidsma.com.

Printed in the United States of America

18 17 16 15 14 5 4 3 2 1

ISBN: 978-1-55570-994-5 (paper).

Library of Congress Cataloging-in-Publication Data

Reidsma, Matthew.
Responsive web design for libraries : a LITA guide / Matthew Reidsma.
pages cm
Includes bibliographical references and index.
ISBN 978-1-55570-994-5 (paper) 1. Library Websites—Design. I. Title.
Z674.75.W67R45 2014
025.0422—dc230 2013051232

Book design in Berkeley and Avenir. Cover image © emEF/Shutterstock, Inc.

⊗ This paper meets the requirements of ANSI/NISO Z39.48-1992 (Permanence of Paper).

Contents

Chapter One

A Case for Responsive Web Design

If you are like me, you spend a lot of time looking at your library website's analytics and server logs. Aside from knowing how many visits your catalog had last week and how many folks left your site after a brief glimpse at your optimistically named FAQ page, you can learn a bit about the people that use your library website and their computers. Sophisticated analytics programs will tell you where your visitors live, what kind of computer they have, and which browser they visited from. Other statistics are squirreled away in these reports, and until recently one particular number didn't differ much from website to website: screen resolution.

This was a boon to website designers. By looking at these statistics, we could tell how large the screens were of our sites' visitors, and thus, we concluded, how big to make our sites. If the data said that our users' screens were 1024 pixels wide and 768 pixels tall, then we were determined to use every glorious pixel of that screen.

Then, in 2007, those reports started to look different. The first iPhone was released, and people could finally browse the web on a phone as easily as they could on a desktop or laptop computer. Our screen resolution reports started to get more diverse, adding screens 320 pixels and 480 pixels wide. Then Google released the Android operating system and the smartphone market exploded; tablets became the new must-have digital gadget; and screens for desktops and laptops changed aspect ratio, from 4:3 to 16:9. Our screen resolution reports now show dozens or hundreds of entries.

This has caused some concern, since we designed our library websites for screens 1024 pixels wide. Our sites were, shall we say, not "optimized" for all these different screens. This sudden influx of different screen sizes has many of us scrambling for a way to make our websites optimized—or even usable—on all of these devices.

And because so many of these devices are "mobile"—touchscreen iPods, smartphones, and tablets large and small—your gut instinct may be to rush out and make a "mobile website" to serve those users. But I'd like to step back for a moment and take a closer look at the full range of challenges that these changes pose for web designers, and for libraries in particular. Once we understand what we're getting ourselves into, then we can better judge our possible paths forward.

A PROLIFERATION OF SCREENS

By the end of 2013, there will be more active mobile devices on the planet than people.[1] That's one cell phone, tablet, or smartphone for every man, woman, and child, the world over. Since the end of 2010, smartphones have outsold traditional desktop and laptop computers,[2] and nearly half of American adults now own a smartphone, an 11 percent increase in just the last year.[3] And this trend looks to continue. Rather than remaining the tool of wealthier socioeconomic classes, smartphone adoption is growing fastest among adults who earn less than $30,000 a year.[4] Although smartphone data plans are more expensive than typical voice and text plans, with the ubiquity and speed of 3G and 4G service a single smartphone represents a savings over separate cell phone and home broadband Internet service.

Teens present a very different picture. Nearly all American teens own a cell phone, and 37 percent of them own smartphones. But half of teen smartphone owners use their phone as their primary way to connect with the Internet. Even those without smartphones are heavy web users. If we include teens with feature phones, one in four uses the Internet primarily from his or her phone.[5]

While smartphones are gaining market share, their own internal diversity is growing. The iPhone went from a 320-by-480 pixel device to a Retina display, in which the physical screen size remained the same but the pixel density doubled. (Then the screen size changed with the iPhone 5.) Android exponentially diversified the device landscape. There are no hard numbers on just how many devices use Android. But in 2012, OpenSignal Maps published data it had collected on the devices that had downloaded its app. It found 1,363 different devices over a six-month period.[6] That's just the reported devices running Android that downloaded one app over a limited period of time.

Even without these data, I can look around the café where I am writing this and see device diversity in action. Nearly half of the folks in this busy coffee shop are looking at or gesticulating with smartphones. I can count a half dozen iPhones and twice as many Android devices. There are more varied screens doodling around the Internet than ever before.

And it's not just smartphones. Tablets are projected to outsell desktop and laptop computers by the end of 2013,[7] and more than 30 percent of American adults own tablets now.[8] A third of smartphone owners also own tablets, and fully 13 percent of all American adults own a smartphone, a tablet, and a desktop or laptop computer.[9]

If you've watched your own analytics, you've probably seen at least some increase in mobile device visits. At Grand Valley State University (GVSU), we went from 1.5 percent of all visits being on a phone or tablet in 2010 to 12 percent of visits by the end of 2013. That's a fivefold increase in visits in just two years, and it won't be letting up anytime soon. The way people connect to the Internet is changing, and sooner or later your library will have to address these changing user needs.

A REALIZATION ABOUT SCREEN DIVERSITY

Although it is certainly true that the diversity of smartphones and tablets has brought the need for better cross-device support to our attention, the problem isn't exactly new. In fact, it's a problem that has been with us all along. When Tim Berners-Lee posted the first HTML page to the Internet, he wasn't concerned with screen size. The text of the page, which is still online today, simply wraps to the width of the user's screen (figure 1.1).[10] The idea of creating a page design based on a minimum width was imported to the web later from the print world, where designers knew how large a finished document would be and designed to fit that size.

The Irish web developer Jeremy Keith, channeling *Neuromancer*, calls our belief that all users view a site at the width of their screen a "consensual hallucination."[11] There has never been a guarantee that anyone viewed our websites at the width of their screens. As the designer Ethan Marcotte pointed out, designing for a screen size is "one step removed from our *actual* canvas: the browser window."[12] We chose to ignore that our sites were viewed at whatever width our patrons set their browser windows until the number of screen sizes simply made this diversity too hard to ignore.

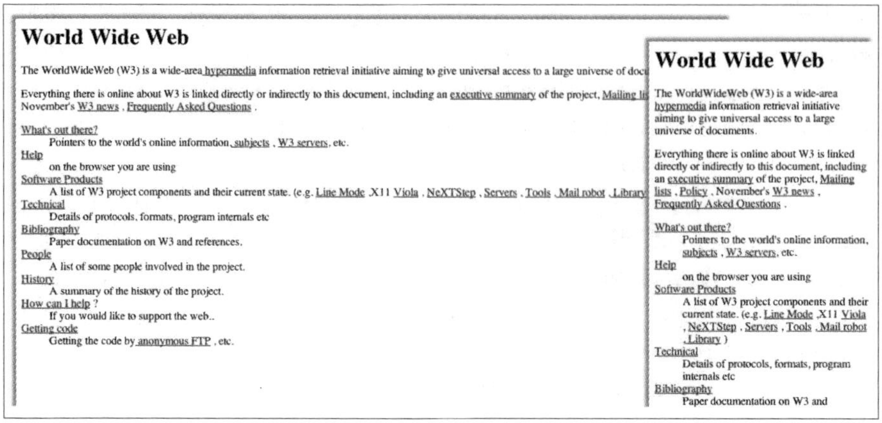

FIGURE 1.1
Tim Berners-Lee's first Web page is naturally fluid, adapting to any screen.

Back in 2000, the designer John Allsopp was already warning us about designing for fixed widths on the web: "The control that designers know in the print medium, and often desire in the web medium, is simply a function of the limitation of the printed page. We should embrace the fact that the web doesn't have the same constraints, and design for this flexibility."[13]

The web is inherently fluid and flexible. We made it fixed and rigid. Rather than trying to deal with more screens by making more rigid, fixed-width mobile sites, what if we worked with the web's nature and thought about it in fluid, flexible terms?

Thankfully, there is a way to build standards-based websites in HTML and CSS that can adapt to any device by thinking responsively.

RESPONSIVE WEB DESIGN DOES NOT MEAN MOBILE WEB SITES

Responsive web design (RWD) differs from creating a "mobile site" in a few ways. A responsive site delivers the same content to all users on the same URL, regardless of the device. Rather than making assumptions about what users on phones, or tablets, or even televisions want to do on your site, serving only the content you *think* they might want, with RWD you serve the same content to everyone.

This may at first go against the prevailing ideas about how people on mobile devices use the web: the rushed businessperson with one eye on the road and the other on his or her phone. Because this mythical mobile user is on the go, logic states that we should assume that the user has a slow network connection and just wants directions to our library or today's hours. But making assumptions about how an entire group of people uses a device is absurd, as designer Mat Marquis pointed out on Twitter: "Mobile users want to see our menu, hours, and delivery number. Desktop users definitely want this 1mb png of someone smiling at a salad."[14]

We seem to accept without reservation that folks browsing on desktop computers all have a variety of needs and desires. Why wouldn't that be true of mobile users? If we look at the data, it turns out that mobile users are as varied as those who are browsing on desktops and laptops.

Rather than using our mobile devices primarily as tools to get point-of-need information when we are on the go, studies show that phone and tablet use is much more diverse. According to a pair of studies from 2010 and 2011, 84 percent of smartphone owners use their devices to browse the web at home, where it is more likely they would be on a high-speed connection.[15] The studies show how well smartphones are at filling downtime, no matter where we are. (Google found that 39 percent of smartphone owners admitted to using them in the bathroom, which might tell us that 61 percent of smartphone owners are liars.)

And far from idle browsing, mobile devices are becoming a tool for getting real work done. In 2011, PayPal handled more than $4 billion in mobile payments,[16] and eBay did more than $5 billion in sales to mobile devices.[17] And eBay isn't tacking up a few billion $1 sales. Each month, the company reports, three to four Ferraris are sold to buyers on mobile devices.[18]

Although separate library mobile sites (or apps) seem attractive, they often don't meet the needs of the users or the teams maintaining them. While a responsive site has one set of content with a single URL, adapting fluidly to fit any device, mobile sites often create additional content management problems. If your hours change, for instance, you might have to update them in two places: one for your desktop site and another for your mobile site. That's a recipe for out-of-date information and unhappy patrons. Even if your CMS can generate templates from a single content source, you'll be generating multiple URLs for each bit of content, depending on whether you are on a mobile device or a desktop computer.

In addition, separate mobile sites often rely on detection scripts to determine whether a visitor should be shown the mobile or the desktop site. These libraries check for mobile-specific browsers or whether the device shows up in a large library of known mobile devices. But with dozens of new mobile devices released each week around the world, keeping these device libraries up to date is a full-time job. What's more, these scripts can't catch every mobile device. When OpenSignal

Maps analyzed its usage data, it found that slightly more than a third of the devices recorded were represented only once, either because they weren't popular or because users had customized the device enough to make its identification unique.

Browser detection is even less reliable. It is trivially easy for browsers to identify themselves however they wish, and because of some bad practices that were common on the web even a few years ago, it is often necessary to trick sites into thinking that your browser is something it is not. These scripts make it hard to be sure the right users are getting to the right site.

RESPONSIVE WEB DESIGN IS FUTURE-FRIENDLY

Maintaining scripts, multiple URLs, templating systems, and various content pools takes staff time, advanced technical skills, and infrastructure—all things in short supply in today's libraries. If you're short on any of these things, than RWD is probably a good solution. Your staff can build one site with the web skills they have now, just semantic HTML and CSS, and focus on making improvements to the services you have rather than fiddling with infrastructure.

Not to mention that mobile-only sites serve a very particular problem that is common now: a proliferation of small screens. But these mobile sites do nothing for devices that will be released in the future with screens or interfaces that aren't small touchscreens. Will we build TV-only sites next year? Google Glass–only sites? Someone in an audience where I recently spoke told me that his new water heater connects to the Internet and has a display. Should we all start building water heater–only sites?

READY OR NOT, THEY ARE ALREADY HERE

The most common response I hear from librarians when I talk about making our sites more accessible to mobile devices is that "no one wants to search the library on their phone." They say this from a place of expertise. I usually remind them of Cliff Stoll, the Internet pioneer who wrote in 1995 that no one in his or her right mind would ever buy anything online.[19] He, too, was an expert, but he wasn't a mind reader.

It is true that buying sports cars and searching for books or articles are different activities. We shouldn't assume that just because some folks are content spending the equivalent of your entire library's technology budget on a car through their phone that this tool is equally as good for research. But the data say that they are already trying.

In 2011, the most common activity smartphone owners reported doing online was searching,[20] so it's not that searching is incompatible with the devices. But general-purpose searching is different from doing research (or at least that's what we've been trying to convince our patrons of for the past century). The good news is that despite the dire predictions of many librarians, people *are* using library websites on mobile devices, or at least they are trying.

I already mentioned that at GVSU traffic from mobile devices accounted for more than 12 percent of visits for 2013. But we aren't an isolated case. According to a Pew Internet and American Life Project study, 39 percent of Americans older than age sixteen have visited a library website at least once, and 25 percent have used a library website in the past year.[21] But more important, 13 percent of Americans older than age sixteen have used a library website on a mobile device in the past year. That's over half of your library's website users in the past year who have at least *tried* to use a phone or tablet to access your online services.

Of course, half of our visits are not coming from mobile devices. Frankly, for many of these users, trying our sites on a mobile device once was enough. Library websites are difficult to use on desktops and laptops, and they are often impossible to use on phones or small tablets. If we want to see an increase in mobile traffic, we're going to need to make it easier for patrons on all devices to use our online services. Would you wait to install a barrier-free entrance until visits from patrons in wheelchairs or walkers increased?

USER EXPECTATIONS ARE CHANGING

The changing landscape of web-enabled devices is causing a shift in the expectations of our users. Most of our library patrons now have the ability to connect to the Internet in their pockets. Where once they might have waited until they were home or at the office to log in and put a hold on an item in the catalog, they can now do this on their phone while on the bus or while waiting at the doctor's office.

When our patrons use our sites in new situations like this, it often highlights the challenges we might have overlooked before. Is your site hard to navigate on a small screen? Patrons might not be able to find their way around while browsing on the phone. Does your catalog require that you log in with your library card barcode? That will be tough to remember while on a crowded bus. These devices are changing the context in which our patrons are interacting with our services, and our websites need to accommodate these quick tasks as well as long research sessions, no matter the device.

In a 2012 survey, Google discovered that 61 percent of smartphone owners will quickly leave a site if it isn't optimized for mobile devices. Forty-eight percent said that websites that weren't optimized for mobile made them feel like the company didn't care about them.[22] In addition, our patrons expect our sites to be faster on mobile devices than on computers. Never mind the slower cellular connections and limited processing power in even the fanciest new smartphone, 60 percent of smartphone owners expect sites to load in three seconds or less on their phones, and 75 percent won't wait more than five seconds.[23]

Needless to say, library websites are not always optimized for speedy performance. But serving up a clunky site meant for a desktop computer to a phone on a slow connection is a recipe for disappointment.

MORE TO DO WITH FEWER RESOURCES

At precisely the time that our patrons are demanding more from our online services, libraries are struggling with budget cuts and staffing shortages. These strains on our libraries are affecting the way we are able to serve our patrons as more and more of our library services come online.

From 2010 to 2012, twenty-three states cut budgets to public libraries, and 40 percent of states have had public library funding cut three years in a row or more.[24] Academic libraries have suffered, too, despite increased enrollments and a nearly 9 percent increase in gate counts since 2008.[25] It takes money to develop and maintain the systems that libraries provide, and shrinking budgets are but one hurdle to overcome. Staffing cuts, particularly at academic libraries, have made it more difficult to add new or improve existing services. Since 2008, academic library staffing levels have fallen by nearly 5 percent.[26]

What's more, many library schools aren't teaching the kind of programming skills necessary to address serious infrastructure problems, and dropping library salaries are sending the talented developers we do have into the private sector.

The challenge, then, is to find a way to make our online services optimized for all of these different devices and contexts while working within shrinking budgets and the restrictions of staff time and skills. Rather than build multiple different interfaces for different devices while maintaining the kind of complex infrastructure to direct each of these users to the right site, we need a way to use our limited time and skills to make our systems work for everyone. Responsive web design lets us build one site for all devices—now and in the future—with just HTML and CSS, skills many of us already have.

SOMETIMES A SEPARATE MOBILE SITE MAKES SENSE, BUT PROBABLY NOT FOR YOU

The case I am making for using responsive web design to build our online services sounds a lot like rainbows and unicorns, so why would anyone build a separate mobile site?

There are times when a separate mobile site makes sense, but generally only when the experience a mobile user needs is completely different from what a desktop user might want. The design firm Happy Cog used to host a karaoke event at the festival South by Southwest called Cog'aoke. The desktop site allowed users to sign up to perform and learn more about their competition. The mobile site, however, had a completely different purpose. The idea was that folks would use the mobile site to vote while at the competition. Because mobile use was seen as a completely different context, the separate mobile site made sense.[27]

But that's probably not what your library needs. If your goal is to serve all of your users with all of the same services, than you need to give everyone the same opportunity to connect to the library online, whether they are visiting on a new MacBook, a nine-year-old Nokia flip phone, or a new water heater.

NOTES

1. Cisco, "Cisco Visual Networking Index: Global Mobile Data Traffic Forecast Update, 2012–2017," www.cisco.com/en/US/solutions/collateral/ns341/ns525/ns537/ns705/ns827/white_paper_c11-520862.html.
2. IDC, "PC Market Records Modest Gains during Fourth Quarter of 2010, according to IDS," January 12, 2011, www.idc.com/about/viewpressrelease.jsp?containerId=prUS22653511&sectionId=null&elementId=null&pageType=SYNOPSIS; IDC, "Android Rises, Symbian^3 and Windows Phone 7 Launch as Worldwide Smartphone Shipments Increase 87.2% Year over Year, according to IDC," February 7, 2011, www.idc.com/about/viewpressrelease.jsp?containerId=prUS22689111&sectionId=null&elementId=null&pageType=SYNOPSIS.
3. Aaron Smith, "Nearly Half of American Adults Are Smartphone Owners," March 1, 2012, www.pewinternet.org/Reports/2012/Smartphone-Update-2012.aspx.
4. Ibid.

5. Brian Hall, "Teenagers & Smartphones: How They're Already Changing the World," April 8, 2013, www.pewinternet.org/Media-Mentions/2013/Teenagers-Smartphones-How-Theyre-Already-Changing-The-World.aspx.

6. OpenSignal, "Android Fragmentation Visualized," August 2012, www.opensignal.com/reports/fragmentation.php.

7. IDC, "Worldwide Smart Connected Device Market Crossed 1 Billion Shipments in 2012, Apple Pulls Near Samsung in Fourth Quarter, according to IDC," March 26, 2013, www.idc.com/getdoc.jsp?containerId=prUS24037713#.UVLzZqsjq5I.

8. Pew Internet & American Life Project, "Trend Data (Adults): Device Ownership," May 2013, www.pewInternet.org/Trend-Data-(Adults)/Device-Ownership.aspx.

9. Leah Christian, Amy Mitchell, and Tom Rosenstiel, "Mobile Devices and News Consumption: Some Good Signs for Journalism," 2012, www.stateofthemedia.org/2012/mobile-devices-and-news-consumption-some-good-signs-for-journalism/.

10. Tim Berners-Lee, "World Wide Web," http://info.cern.ch/hypertext/WWW/TheProject.html.

11. Jeremy Keith, "Context," March 27, 2011, http://adactio.com/journal/4443/.

12. Ethan Marcotte, *Responsive Web Design* (New York: A Book Apart, 2011), 3.

13. John Allsopp, "A Dao of Web Design," April 7, 2000, http://alistapart.com/articles/dao.

14. Mat Marquis, @wilto, April 27, 2011, www.twitter.com/wilto/status/63284673723375616.

15. Danielle Bulger, "Smartphone Owners: A Ready and Willing Audience," March 12, 2010, http://blog.compete.com/2010/03/12/smartphone-owners-a-ready-and-willing-audience/; Google, "Complimentary Copy of 'Mobile Movement: Understanding Smartphone Users' Study," April 28, 2011, http://googlemobileads.blogspot.com/2011/04/complimentary-copy-of-mobile-movement.html.

16. Danielle Kucera, "eBay's PayPal Mobile Payment Volume Rose to $4 Billion Last Year," *BloombergBusinessweek*, January 11, 2012, www.businessweek.com/news/2012-01-11/ebay-s-paypal-mobile-payment-volume-rose-to-4-billion-last-year.html.

17. Leena Rao, "eBay Forecasts $8B in Mobile Commerce Volume in 2012; PayPal Will Reach $7B," January 12, 2012, www.techcrunch.com/2012/01/12/ebay-forecasts-8b-in-mobile-commerce-volume-in-2012-paypal-will-reach-7b/.

18. Liane Yvkoff, "Fancy a Ferrari? Rev Up eBay Motors Mobile App," February 3, 2011, http://reviews.cnet.com/8301-13746_7-20030552-48.html.

19. Stoll's argument was that "what's missing from sales over a network . . . [is] a real person who will respond to my needs." Cliff Stoll, *Silicon Snake Oil*, (New York: Doubleday, 1995), 105–6.

20. Google, "Complimentary Copy of 'Mobile Movement: Understanding Smartphone Users' Study," April 28, 2011, http://googlemobileads.blogspot.com/2011/04/complimentary-copy-of-mobile-movement.html.

21. What is not clear from this study is how the respondents understood what the "library website" was. If your catalog is online, for instance, then 100 percent of patrons who use the catalog have used the library website but not realized it. Maeve Duggan, Lee Rainie, and Kathryn Zickuhr, "Mobile Connections to Libraries," December 31, 2012, http://libraries.pewInternet.org/2012/12/31/mobile-connec tions-to-libraries/.
22. Google, "Mobile-Friendly Sites Turn Visitors into Customers," September 25, 2012, http://googlemobileads.blogspot.com/2012/09/mobile-friendly-sites-turn-visitors .html.
23. Compuware, "Survey Report: 'What Users Want from Mobile,'" https://web.archive .org/web/20130310221542/http://www.gomez.com/resources/whitepapers/survey -report-what-users-want-from-mobile/.
24. American Library Association, "Public Libraries," http://ala.org/news/mediapress center/americaslibraries/soal2012/public-libraries.
25. American Library Association, "Academic Libraries," http://ala.org/news/mediapress center/americaslibraries/soal2012/academic-libraries.
26. Ibid.
27. I learned about the Cog'aoke site in Ethan Marcotte's talk on responsive design at the An Event Apart conference in Boston, Massachusetts, on May 2, 2011.

Chapter Two

Fluid Layouts

We're seeing more kinds of devices doing more things on the web every day, but most of us are still building websites the way we did for desktop computers on dial-up connections a decade ago. We need to get clear about the different ways in which we lay out websites and which techniques are appropriate to the web and a multidevice world.

LAYOUT IS AN ENHANCEMENT

It's hard to imagine a web page that doesn't have a visual layout. In the library world, we spend a lot of time shuffling users between different online systems: our catalog, consortium catalogs, vendor databases, and more. We instruct folks using one database to click a button on the "left side of the screen," whereas users of another database will find that button on the "right side." We're forever giving instructions for our online tools based on how those sites are visually arranged. We rarely perceive the content separated from the layout.

But the web didn't start with any way to add visual layouts to web pages. How HTML looked in a browser reflected the semantic organization of the content: headings, lists, and paragraphs.

Despite maturing for more than two decades, HTML is still a markup language for structuring documents. Its elements have semantic meaning, whereas the visual differences they exhibit are a product of their function in the document rather than a way to express visual layout. That HTML elements have been used by themselves to create all manner of sophisticated layouts is because of the creativity (some might say unorthodoxy) of many of the web's earliest "designers."

Boston-based designer Ethan Marcotte reminds us that layout is an enhancement rather than a fundamental part of the web. More than twenty years into the web, this sounds crazy, since we often think of web pages as how they appear visually.

But HTML has never comfortably accepted layout elements. The `<table>` element, which has functioned as the basic layout grid of most websites since the mid-1990s, is a tool for displaying tabular data in rows and columns. It was later hijacked to build the scaffolding on which visual layouts were created. Other elements designed for display have been deprecated with the maturity and wide adoption of Cascading Style Sheets (CSS): the `<center>` and `<font>` elements chief among them. In fact, the decades-old rallying cry from the Web Standards Project to separate structure (HTML) from presentation (CSS) is itself convincing evidence that HTML is a semantic markup language for structuring documents rather than a tool for placing content elements in specific locations on a canvas. If designers want a button to appear on the left-hand side of the user's screen, they should use CSS, not HTML.

Except now even that idea is being complicated by the current and future landscape of devices connecting to the web. The left side of which screen, exactly? We can't be certain of which kind of screen our users are going to view our sites on next. And because our mission as libraries is to offer our services to anyone and everyone, we need to make sure that we take care in building websites that will work on any web-enabled device, today and in the future. On the web, not everyone is so thoughtful.

The Florida Division of Emergency Management website (www.floridadisaster.org) is a clearinghouse of information for Florida residents in the case of upcoming or current disasters. Not just anyone can view this site, though. There is a whole page devoted to the requirements for using the site: which browsers to use and which additional applications you must install to access much of the content, which is locked away in PDFs and Flash videos (figure 2.1). Also, the site recommends a monitor with a resolution of at least 1024 pixels by 768 pixels. When are you likely to look for information during a disaster? When sitting at a desk with a large computer monitor, or while running out the door with your phone in hand?

In contrast, the *Boston Globe* website (www.bostonglobe.com) is built to separate structure from presentation. By beginning with a strong, standards-based foundation of HTML and then adding layout as an enhancement with CSS, the *Globe* website works on any device that can render HTML, even a fifteen-year old Apple Newton, as Grant Hutchinson demonstrated.[1] Although visitors to our

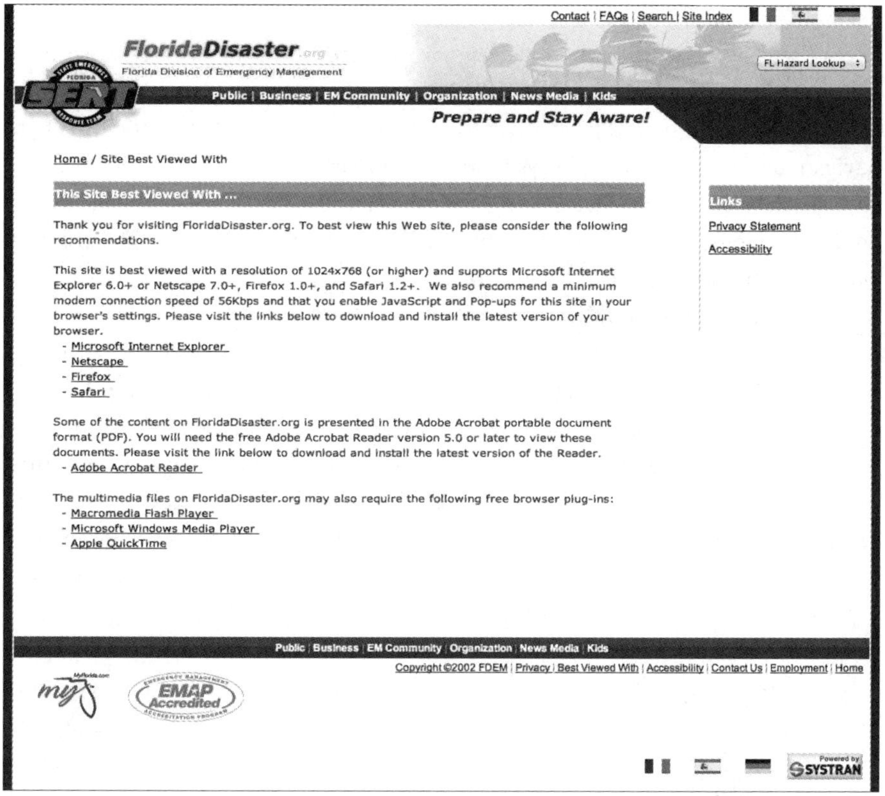

FIGURE 2.1

Florida Division of Emergency Management website.

library websites might not be browsing on vintage electronics, they are using feature phones, smartphones, new and old desktop and laptop computers, televisions, and whatever else will connect to the web over the next few years. By treating layout as an enhancement, we can make sure our sites are ready for any device our users currently have, as well as whatever devices they won't be able to live without in the future. To paraphrase designer Trent Walton, our websites should meet our users where they are.[2]

DESIGNING SOURCE ORDER

Designers have been calling for a separation of structure and presentation in web design for the past fifteen years, but the argument is usually about moving styles out of markup and into CSS. There are other presentational elements to consider.

Take navigation, those elements of a website that help you browse around a site to find what you need. Early on, designers latched on to the list elements <ul> and <ol> to markup navigation. This was an appropriate semantic choice, since navigation is often nested lists of pages, like an outline or table of contents. These navigation lists were almost always found in the markup right after the first heading or logo, despite the fact that putting navigation at the top of a document doesn't have a semantic purpose. Instead, placing navigation at the top of the markup was a presentational choice. Navigation is often found at the top of a web page in a visual layout, so it would often be placed in the document where it was to be rendered visually.

Although no presentational elements were used, this is still using HTML for layout. In contrast, CSS lets us position elements almost anywhere, regardless of where they fall structurally within the markup. There is no need to make the source order of our document represent the visual layout, and in fact there are many reasons to avoid this practice. It causes problems for users who never experience our visual layouts, such as those who are visually impaired or those with less capable devices, making them sift through long navigational lists just to get what they came for: our content.

Of course, accessibility work-arounds for this problem exist. The most common is to include an anchor link at the top of the page that lets you skip the navigation and get right to the content. This link is "seen" by screen readers and other assistive devices (as well as less capable devices without CSS support) but is hidden from browsers that can render a visual layout. Since our users come to our sites for the content, I prefer placing our content first and offering an anchor link to the navigation for assistive devices. This way all users can get to our content quickly, and those who need to use our navigation can do so easily. Meanwhile, we leave all aspects of our visual design to the CSS, where it belongs.

Let's see how this works in action. Pretend you've been given a simple wireframe for a library website and have been asked to turn it into semantic HTML (figure 2.2).

While you might be tempted to start arranging content into <div>s or (heaven forbid) <table> cells, let's take a step back and do an inventory of our content. Since we need to build a semantic HTML document that will serve as the framework on which we place our visual design, it's important to think about our content and how our users will relate to it. We want the most important stuff to be first. Here is a list of what our mockup has, from top to bottom, left to right:

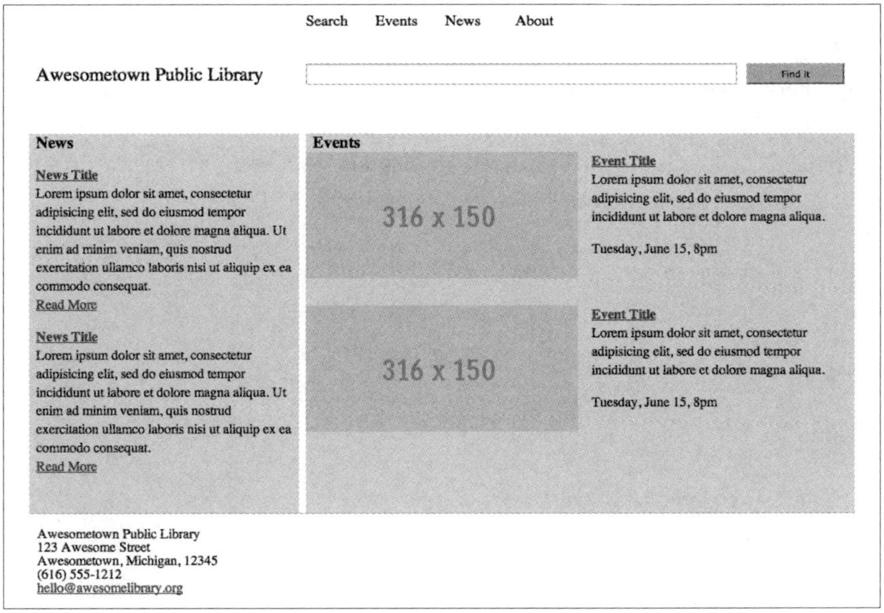

FIGURE 2.2
A simple wireframe for our library website.

- navigation
- logo
- search form
- news stories (two, with text)
- in-library events (two images with text)
- footer with contact information and additional links

When we think about why our users come to our site, some of these items might be too high or low in the hierarchy. For instance, no one comes primarily for our navigation, yet visually it is given more priority than news, which along with the search box, is relevant to all users, whether or not they are physically able to attend our events or exhibits. A revised hierarchical list would look like this:

1. Logo
2. Search form
3. News stories (two, with text)

4. In-library events (two images with text)
5. Navigation
6. Footer with contact information and additional links

We can then translate this content hierarchy into markup (I'm leaving out some elements and attributes to make the code a bit more readable):

```
<div id="page">
    <h1>Awesometown Public Library</h1>
    <form>
        <input type="text" name="search" />
        <input type="submit" value="Find it" />
    </form>
    <div role="main">
        <div class="left"> … </div>
        <div class="right"> … </div>
    </div><!-- end [role=main] -->
    <div role="navigation">
        <ol> … </ol>
    </div><!-- end #navigation -->
    <div id="footer" role="complimentary"> … </div>
</div><!-- end #page -->
```


Now we have some well-structured HTML that presents our content first to any web-enabled device (if we had content). By designing our source order to emphasize the importance of the content for our library's users, we've been able to fully separate structure from presentation. We can now start thinking about enhancing the experience of using our site for more capable devices, like those that support CSS.

Not every project will begin with a redesign or a comprehensive visual mockup. If you already have a library website and restructuring markup isn't an option, don't worry. At GVSU, I built our responsive website around our campus content management system, which meant that I didn't have control over the source order of anything in the campus template: headers, navigation, or footers. (I'm happy to say that now our university template's navigation is near the end of the source order.) In the last half of the book, I'll show you some strategies for implementing responsive design on your existing website.

GRID-BASED LAYOUTS

Once we move from the structure of the document to the presentation, we face more challenges than just writing clean code. How will we organize the content visually so that it makes sense for users? And crucially, what does it mean to create a visual layout in an ever-expanding multidevice world?

Having a logical system for organizing our visual layout is important, since we need a way to determine how our layout will adapt for different devices. By starting with a structured layout, we can better adapt our visual rules for different screen sizes, orientations, ratios, and dimensions. The typographic grid is the perfect design tool, aimed to help designers organize content visually in a precise and logical way. Popularized in the early twentieth century by Jan Tschichold, the typographic grid acts like an invisible scaffolding, proportionally dividing the page into rows and columns, onto which content is placed.[3]

To build a grid, we want to divide our site into equal vertical grid units, separated by gutters. Ideally, we want these units to be multiples of three or four, because we'll have more flexibility in our layout. Twelve units is perfect, since it is a multiple of both three and four, and allows for a lot of flexibility. With twelve grid units we can align our content as two columns of six units each, three columns of four units each, four columns of three units each, or six columns of two units each (figure 2.3).

Unfortunately, we can't just use the same grid for every project, because our site has constraints that we need to account for when building our grid. In our case, we have the constraint of the images, which are 316 pixels wide. These constraints can help us develop a grid, since we know the dimensions of our canvas and those of a constraint. In addition, we know that our content will be presented in three columns, so we know that our grid units need to be divisible by 3. Finding the best value can be a bit of trial and error, so let's think through how we might divide up our grid by examining the width of our images.

First, let's break down our image into column units. Let's try for a twelve-unit grid first, which would mean that our image would need to be split into four column units with three gutters. There is a formula that can help us figure out our unit widths, shared by the designers Khoi Vinh and Mark Boulton:[4]

$$\text{Canvas} - [(\text{Total Units} - 1) \times \text{Gutter}] \div \text{Total Units} = \text{Unit Width}$$

Here our canvas is 316 pixels, the width of our image. We'll need to try out different gutter sizes to find one that works, but in this case let's try 10 pixels. Our formula looks like:

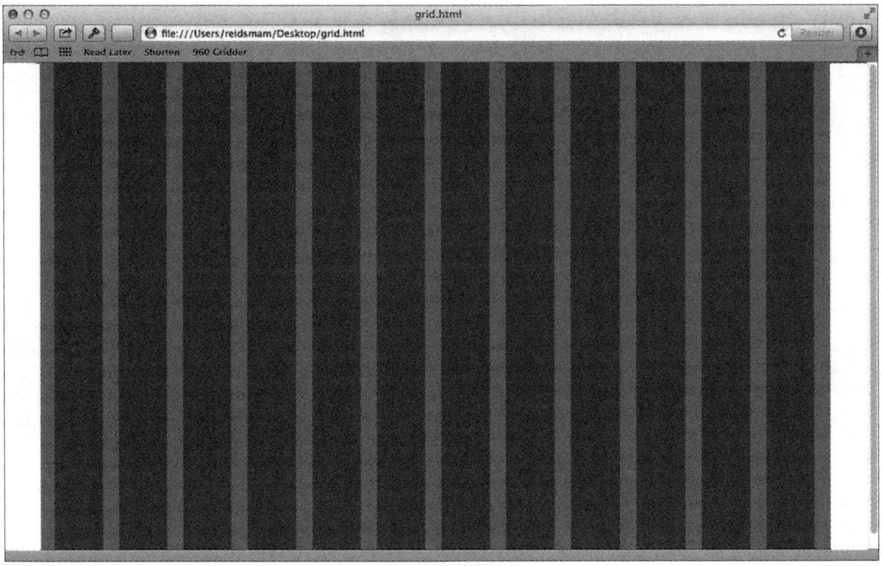

FIGURE 2.3
Nice grid, but where is the content?

$$316 - [(4 - 1) \times 10] \div 4 = 71.5$$

We can't have grid units that measure to the half pixel, so that won't work. We'll either need to change the number of grid units in our grid or change the value of our gutter.

Let's try making our gutters just a bit smaller, say 8 pixels:

$$316 - [(4 - 1) \times 8] \div 4 = 73$$

It worked! Our 316-pixel image will sit atop four 73-pixel grid units separated by 8-pixel gutters (figure 2.4). Going back to our wireframe, we'll have three of

FIGURE 2.4
Our grid is tailored
to fit design constraints.

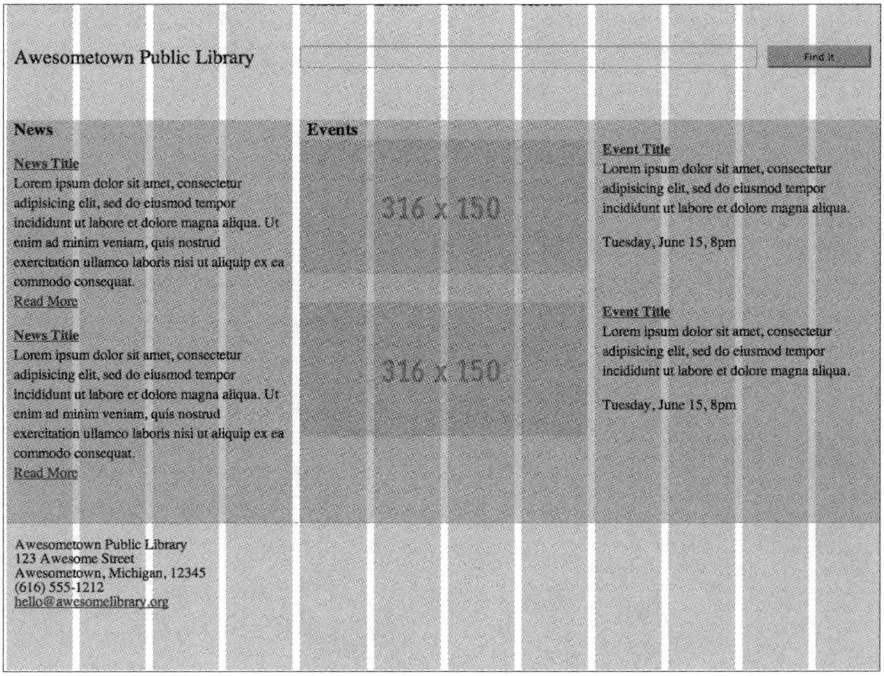

FIGURE 2.5
Our grid-based layout, now with grid!

these columns, each separated by another 8-pixel gutter, so our whole page will be 964 pixels, divided into twelve grid units (figure 2.5).

With our fixed-width grid configured, we can now find the width of every element in our layout and start writing CSS. Here are the big chunks:

```
#page {
     margin: 0 auto;
     width: 964px;
}
h1 {
     float: left;
     width: 316px; /* 3 grid units & 2 gutters */
}
form#search {
     float: left;
     width: 640px; /* 6 grid units & 5 gutters */
}
.left {
     float: left;
```

```
    width: 316px; /* 3 grid units & 2 gutters */
}
.right {
    float: right;
    width: 640px; /* 6 grid units & 5 gutters */
}
```

Despite it's lack of color and appropriate typography, our website now has a genuine, proportional layout (except for that pesky navigation). But since I went through all of the trouble of convincing you that navigation should be at the end of the source order, we'll move our navigation to the top of the visual layout with CSS. The process is rather simple, and was discovered a while back by the designer Raphaël Goetter and popularized by Jeremy Keith.[5] Although using tables in our markup to control layout is still evil, using CSS to display elements *like* tables is not. We're going to tell the body element to act like a table, and then set the navigation as the table's caption. We just need a few CSS declarations:


```
body {
    caption-side: top;
    display: table;
}
[role="navigation"] {
    display: table-caption;
    margin-left:
}
[role="navigation"] ol {
    display: table-row;
}
[role="navigation"] ol li {
    display: table-cell;
    padding-right: 8px; /* width of a gutter */
    width: 73px; /* The width of one grid unit */
}
```

Now our website is starting to look like the wireframe we were given earlier. If our browser window drops below 964 pixels wide, the width of `#page`, we lose some of the content in our right column.

Building this grid around a fixed constraint led us to fix the width of our page to 964 pixels. If we want our design to adapt to any screen size, larger or smaller than we intended, we'll need to rethink how we calculate our constraints when we created our grid. Our grid should define the proportional relationships among our content modules, rather than fixed dimensions and positions. We need our fixed grid to be more fluid.

FROM FIXED-WIDTH TO FLUID GRIDS

Even if you have never used a grid to create visual layouts before, if you've ever worked on the web, the previous section probably seemed familiar. You set a fixed width on your content's containing element (in our case, `#page`), and then set the positioning and pixel widths of each of its descendants. But since we want our layout to flex and adapt, we need to build our containers and columns proportionately.

Fortunately, converting a fixed-width layout to a proportional one is simply a matter of math. Since we know the widths of our content elements as well as the width of their container (`#page`), we can determine the proportional relationship between each column and its container. Let's look at a real-world example of how this works.

Imagine that you have a container of eggs in your refrigerator that can hold a dozen eggs. However, if we're honest, you don't remember how many eggs are in there (or when you bought them, for that matter). If you opened up the container and found six eggs, you'd know that the container was half full. You wouldn't need to do any math to prove this, probably, but let's do it so we can see how it works. First, we need to know the size of the container, in this case, how many egg slots our container has: twelve. Then we need to divide the number of eggs we actually have, six, by the size of the container:

$$6 \div 12 = .5 \ (50\%)$$

The percentage we get from this formula is an expression of the relationship between the number of eggs we have and the size of our container. We could use this same formula to calculate this relationship as a percentage no matter how many eggs we had left. For instance, if we had seven eggs left, we would have a slightly less friendly percentage representing the relationship between our eggs and their container:

$$7 \div 12 = .5833333333 \ (58.3333333\%)$$

By dividing the fixed number of eggs by the fixed number of egg slots in our container, we represent this relationship in proportional terms rather than fixed ones. If this were a book about responsive baking, I might be able to wrap this chapter up now. Instead, let's make the leap from eggs to websites.

We can use this same formula to convert our fixed pixel-width columns to proportional percentages, simply by dividing the width of our content elements in pixels by the total number of "pixel slots" in their container. Ethan Marcotte, in his book *Responsive Web Design*, expressed the formula like this:[6]

Target ÷ Context = Result

In this case, our target is the pixel value of our content element and the context is the containing element. Let's start with our logo, the `<h1>` element. In our fixed-width mockup, the `<h1>` is 316 pixels wide, and its containing element is `#page`, which is 964 pixels wide. We'll plug these into the formula to get the following:

316 ÷ 964 = 0.32780082987552

Well, that's not a very friendly number. To convert this to a percentage, we can multiply it by 100, to get 32.780082987552 percent. This means that the first header is 32.780082987552 percent of the total page width. While we might be tempted to round that value up to 33 percent, don't bother. Computers are much better with numbers than we are, and we want to express the proportional relationship between this element and it's parent as specifically as possible.

The search form spans eight grid units, for 640 pixels. We can use the same formula (Target ÷ Context = Result) formula to calculate the proportional relationship of the search form to the container:

640 ÷ 964 = 0.66390041493776, or 66.390041493776%

We can use this formula to calculate the proportional value of all of the content elements and replace the fixed pixel values in our CSS with our newly calculated percentages:

```
h1 {
     float: left;
     width: 32.780082987552%;
     /* 316 / 964 = 0.32780082987552 */
}
form#search {
     float: left;
     width: 66.390041493776%;
     /* 640 / 964 = 0.66390041493776 */
```

```
}
.left {
     float: left;
     width: 32.780082987552%;
     /* 316 / 964 = 0.32780082987552 */
}
.right {
     float: right;
     width: 66.390041493776%;
     /* 640 / 964 = 0.66390041493776 */
}
```

If we change these values, our layout looks exactly the same as it did before, but it also remains inflexible, because we have a declared pixel width on the parent element, `<body>`. We can make our layout flexible by simply changing this fixed width on our parent to a proportional one. Since our wireframe assumed a screen size of 1024 pixels, we can use our trusty formula to find the proportional value of the `<body>` element compared to the imagined width of the browser window:

$$964 \div 1024 = 0.94140625\ (94.140625\%)$$

By then changing our container's CSS, we can make the whole layout flexible (figure 2.6):

```
#page {
     width: 94.140625%; /* 964 / 1024 = 0.94140625 */
}
```

Our layout flexes when the browser window is resized, and it looks pretty good (except for a few things that squish together). But element width is only one part of our design. We need to add appropriate margins and padding to finish off our basic layout.

FLEXIBLE MARGINS AND PADDING

The CSS box model is a little screwy, and that can make declaring flexible margins and padding difficult. In the standard box model, padding is calculated as something in addition to the width of the element. If we have a box that is

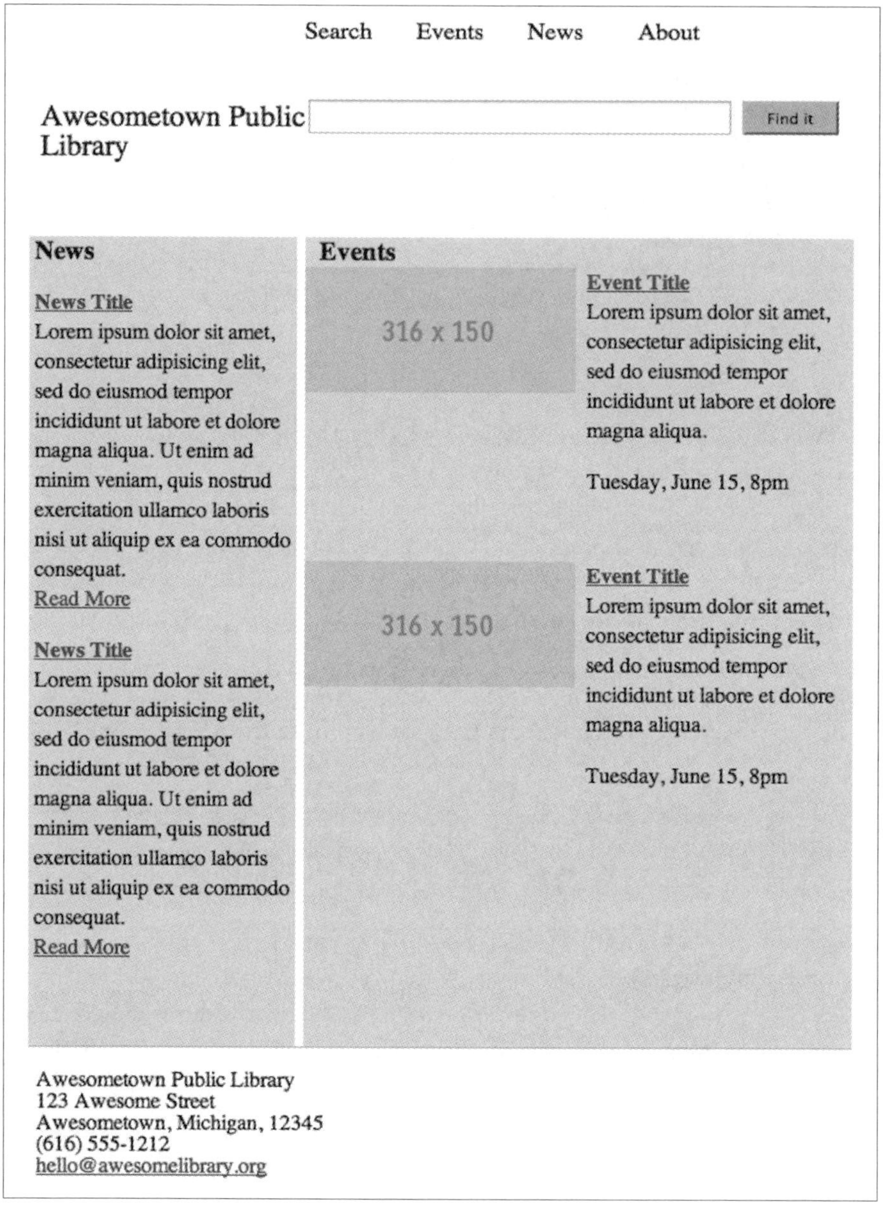

FIGURE 2.6

Now that our layout is fluid, we don't hide content from users when the browser window changes.

250 pixels wide and we add 10 pixels of padding to the left and right, we then have a box that is 270 pixels wide. This means that if we add padding to those proportional widths we just calculated, our content elements will all bloat up with added size.

Happily, there is a better way. We can ask the browser to stop using the screwy CSS box model and instead apply any declared padding inside of the element without affected the width of the element. Simply add this CSS to your elements:

```
-moz-box-sizing: border-box;
-webkit-box-sizing: border-box;
box-sizing: border-box;
```

Now, if we declare an element to be 250 pixels wide, and we add 10 pixels of padding, the element is still 250 pixels wide. The padding it added *inside* of the box.

Browser support for `box-sizing: border-box` is strong, although we'll need some work-arounds for Internet Explorer 8 and below, which I'll cover in chapter 5.

Now we can calculate flexible margins and padding without worrying about adding bloat. However, the context we'll use to determine proportional widths is different for padding than for margins. The context for fluid margins is the width of the containing element, as expected. But the context for fluid padding is the width of the element itself. Let's add 10 pixels of padding to our columns with our trusty formula.

Since our context for padding is the width of the element, `.left`'s context is 316 pixels, and `.right`'s is 640 pixels. Our CSS with fluid padding looks like this:

```
.left {
     float: left;
     padding: 1em 3.164556962025%;
     /* 10 / 316 = 0.03164556962025 */
     width: 32.780082987552%;
}
.right {
     float: right;
     padding: 1em 1.5625%; /* 10/ 640 = 0.015625 */
     width: 66.390041493776%;
}
```

Even though both columns have the same fixed value of padding applied, 10 pixels, the proportional values differ because each has it's own context.

FLEXIBLE FONT SIZING

If we want to build truly fluid websites in which elements are sized proportionately, then we need to also consider font sizing. Generally, we size fonts with pixels, but that's not very flexible. Some older browsers have trouble zooming text that is declared in pixels, and that's an accessibility problem we want to avoid. (After all, we have a large-print book section—why not let those folks use our website in large print?) So how do we move to proportional sizing with fonts? We use a proportional value, the em, instead of pixels.

In addition to scaling properly, using ems has a workflow benefit for us. Because ems are proportional to the `font-size` of their container, by resizing the outmost container's `font-size`, all fonts on our page will be resized to match. This can be really handy when your boss asks you to make the default `font-size` of every bit of text a little bigger. Instead of fixing every single `font-size` declaration in pixels, you can just change one CSS declaration. Let's see how this works by sizing our `<h1>` in ems. But first we'll make a small change to our `<h1>` markup, adding a `<span>` that has a smaller `font-size` than the rest of the text:

```
<h1>
    Awesometown Public Library
    <span>It's the best</span>
</h1>
h1 {
    float: left;
    font-size: 48px;
    width: 32.780082987552%;
}
h1 span {
    font-size: 32px;
}
```

To size our `<h1>` proportionately, we first need to declare a base `font-size` for the whole document by setting the `font-size` of the `<body>` element to 100 percent. By default, most browsers default `font-size` is 16 pixels, so by declaring our outermost container's `font-size` to 100 percent, we've made 1 em equal to

16 pixels. Let's bring back our formula for calculating proportional values to help us make our fonts more flexible. Since the context of our heading is its container's `font-size`, our context will be 16 pixels. So for our `<h1>` we have:

48 ÷ 16 = 3

Our `<h1>` font size is going to be 3 ems. Now we can calculate the same proportional value of our `<span>`, but we have to consider that our context has changed, because the containing element for the `<span>` is our `<h1>`, not `<body>`. So the `font-size` of the context is 48 pixels, the fixed size of our `<h1>`.

32 ÷ 48 = .666666667

The proportional size of our `<span>` is .666666667 ems. Our revised, proportional CSS is now:

```
body {
    font-size: 100%;
}
h1 {
    float: left;
    font-size: 3em;
    width: 32.780082987552%;
}
h1 span {
    font-size: .666666667em;
}
```

In the last section, I declared vertical padding in our `.left` and `.right` containers in ems rather than in percentages. By using ems, we can declare fixed vertical padding and margins that are proportional to the container's `font-size`.

FLEXIBLE IMAGES AND MEDIA

So far we've built a pretty straightforward flexible grid. Widths, fonts, padding, and margins are all expressed proportionately. We're ready to drop some content into our shiny new library site. Unfortunately, the content your boss hands us to fill up our newly flexible layout is anything but fluid. Bitmap image files and downright inflexible embedded video. Why did we waste all of that time making things flexible when we're just going to fill them up with inflexible content? Luckily, we can help inflexible content such as images and video become fluid. Our work was not in vain!

Let's take a look at the markup for our events in the `.right` column (» added for line wraps):

```
<h3>Events</h3>
<div class="event-img">
    <img src="/img/awesome-event.png" »
      alt="Inflexible image" />
</div>
```

This inflexible image your boss sent us is 450 pixels wide, but it is only supposed to span three grid units, so we'll use our little formula to figure out the width and apply a little CSS and hope that the image behaves by sizing its containing element, `.event-img`:

```
.event-img {
    float: left;
    width: 49.375%; /* 316px ÷ 640px = 0.49375 */
}
```


Unfortunately, since our image is much wider than `.event-img`, it boldly spreads itself out of its container and off to the right, across the text (figure 2.7). We could resize the image to the exact pixel dimensions our wireframe calls for, but that still wouldn't help us when the site is viewed at any width above or below the imaginary window width our wireframe is based on.

What we need is a way to constrain the image's width within its container. We want it to behave more like the fluid text on the web page. Thankfully, Richard Rutter shared just such a trick years ago, and all it takes is a simple rule:[7]

```
img {
    max-width: 100%;
}
```

With that one simple CSS rule, all of our images will resize themselves to fit within their parent elements. In this case, our image will never be larger that 100 percent of the parent element, `.event-img.` That despair you were feeling when your images ran wild over your flexible layout? It should be mostly gone.

Except we still have one more inflexible layout dragon to slay. We need to embed a video into our markup using an `<iframe>. HTML <video>` elements work fine with `max-width: 100%` just like images, but `<iframe>s` do not. While browsers can comfortably scale images while maintaining the correct aspect

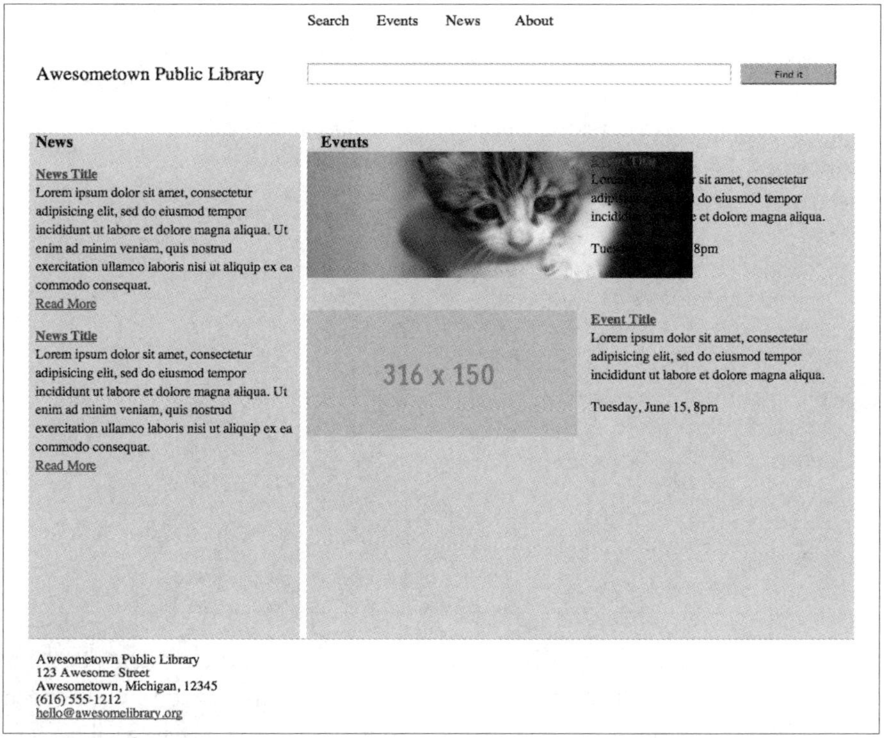

FIGURE 2.7
That's not quite what we had in mind.

ratio, `<iframe>` heights are not adjusted when the width changes. Fortunately, another smart designer solved this back in 2009. Thierry Koblentz developed a technique for tricking browsers into preserving a video's aspect ratio by wrapping it in something that does scale correctly: an HTML containing element.[8]

Here is the markup we'll start with:

```
<div class="video-wrapper">
    <iframe width="560" height="315"
src="http://www.youtube.com/embed/...">
    </iframe>
</div><!-- end .video-wrapper -->
```

We calculate the aspect ratio of the video, in this case 16:9, as a percentage: 9 ÷ 16 = 56.25 percent. Then we'll create vertical padding below our element with a height proportionally tied to the aspect ratio. Then we'll position the `<iframe>` video into this padding area, since we didn't leave any room for content in our element. Since an aspect ratio is simply the proportional relationship between the width and height of an object, we've tied the value of the container's height to its width. When the width changes, the height will change proportionally. Because we're filling this container with our video, its height and width with scale fluidly, just like our images:

```
.video-wrapper {
     height: 0;
     padding-bottom: 56.25%; /* 16:9 */
     position: relative;
}
.video-wrapper iframe {
     position: absolute;
     top: 0;
     left: 0;
     right: 0;
     bottom: 0;
}
```


Now we have a fluid, grid-based layout, and even a little content. But this simplified example of creating fluid grid-based layouts isn't everything we need to know to build truly responsive, not just fluid, websites. For that, we'll need to add media queries.

NOTES

1. Grant Hutchinson, "HTML5 vs Newton: *The Boston Globe*," Flickr, www.flickr.com/photos/splorp/6141222275.
2. Trent Walton, "Fit to Scale," http://trentwalton.com/2011/05/10/fit-to-scale/.
3. See especially his 1928 classic, *The New Typography*, which has been brought back into print in the past few decades by several publishers.
4. Mark Boulton and Khoi Vinh, "Grids are Good (Right?)," March 10, 2007, www.subtraction.com/pics/0703/grids_are_good.pdf.
5. Jeremy Keith, "Re-tabulate," August 16, 2011, http://adactio.com/journal/4780.
6. Ethan Marcotte, *Responsive Web Design* (New York: A Book Apart, 2011), 20.
7. Richard Rutter, "Image Test 3," *clagnut* (blog), http://clagnut.com/sandbox/imagetest3/.
8. Thierry Koblentz, "Creating Intrinsic Ratios for Video," May 26, 2009, http://alistapart.com/articles/creating-intrinsic-ratios-for-video.

Chapter Three

Media Queries

In the last chapter, we converted our fixed-width layout to a fluid, percentage-based grid that didn't hide content from our users when they visited our site with a screen or browser window smaller than the size of our original mockup. If we resize the browser window a little, making it a little smaller or a little bigger than our design intended, our layout nicely flexes and condenses, retaining the proportions of our original design. But if we resize our browser window radically—making it as small as possible or twice as big as intended—then our design starts to show its weaknesses. On the small end, the proportional columns are too small for the content to easily fit, and on the large end, the lines of text will be too long to read comfortably (figure 3.1). Even though the layout is fluid, this isn't enough to accommodate the whole range of screen sizes that will potentially visit our site. We need a way to further adapt our layouts to serve different devices, beyond just making our site fluid.

THE VIEWPORT

So far we've spent a lot of time talking about screen sizes and browser windows, because in designing websites we've often been guilty of assuming a common, shared width at which all of our users view our sites. And while today's mobile devices generally show web pages the full width of the screen, that "width" changes with the orientation of the device. An iPhone 3GS held in portrait has a width of

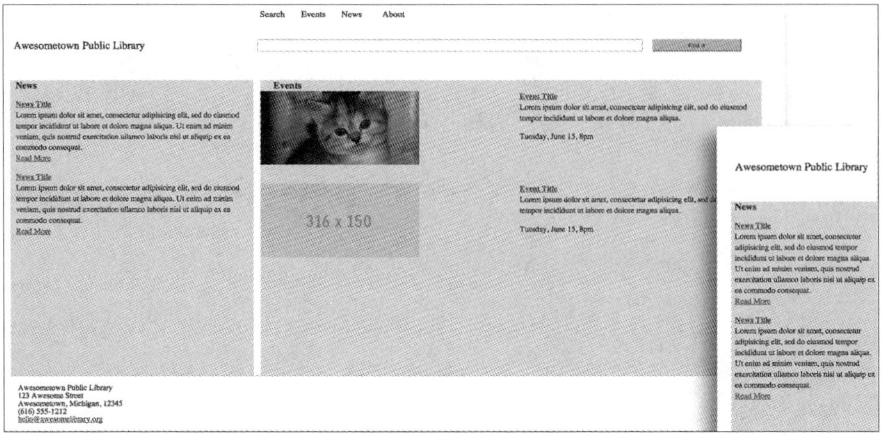

FIGURE 3.1
When the browser window is small, everything is smushed.
Too large and everything is unreadable.

320 pixels, but when switched to landscape, the width switches to 480 pixels. The iPhone 4's Retina display changes the effective widths to 640 pixels or 960 pixels, although it assumes that sites are not optimized for the higher-density screens, which further complicates things. And that's just two models of one type of phone from one manufacturer. Add in the zillions of Android phones and tablets, and it quickly becomes clear that we're dealing with a host of unknowns when it comes to device screen size.

But remember, uncertainty has always existed, even before the explosion of mobile devices made us question designing for a fixed-width screen. In the preceding chapters, I've used the terms *browser window* when talking about the size of a site displayed on a desktop computer and *screen size* when talking about mobile devices. On mobile devices, the screen size and browser window are one and the same thing (at least now), even though the screen "size" is flexible depending on orientation and pixel density. The size of the window in which our users see our sites has always been controlled by the user, constrained only by the screen resolution.

There is a term in software development that describes the window in which our browser appears: the *viewport*. Instead of qualifying whether our site is viewed at screen width, as on a mobile device, or browser-window width, as on a desktop or laptop computer, the viewport describes both. It simply refers to the height and width of the software, and the term was adopted early on in the development

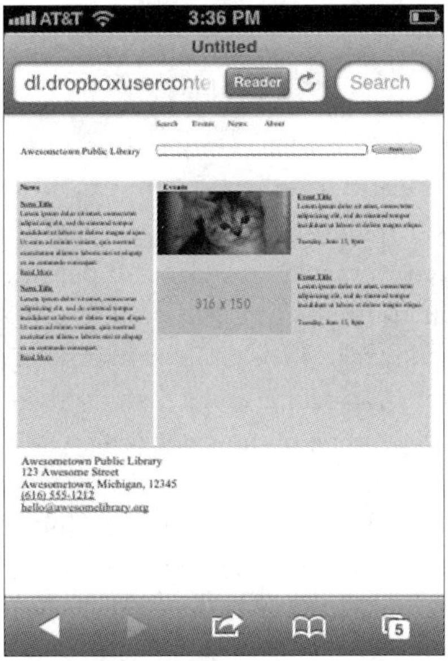

Figure 3.2
Even though our site is fluid, it doesn't adapt to the phone's screen.

of the first iPhone to help avoid the ambiguity inherent in the constantly variable dimensions that were common to how the iPhone (and now, basically all smartphones) render websites.

Because most websites are designed for fixed-width screens around 1000 pixels wide, the designers of mobile Safari developed an algorithm for rendering the full width of a website in the confined 320- or 480-pixel-wide screen of the phone. The site would appear to be zoomed out, often with text too small to read and links too small to click. But by showing the entire site at a glance, users would be able to find the content they wanted. By using finger gestures to zoom in, the user can interact with the website.

If we load our wireframe page on a phone now with our fluid grid, the site will still render as if it were designed for desktop computers, forcing us to pinch and zoom to read the text (figure 3.2).

But Mobile Safari's designers wanted us to be able to create sites that were optimized for the width of the new phone. They created a new `<meta>` element that lets us set the width of the viewport, the ratio at which the page is scaled, and a few other options. In short, it lets us make pages that don't appear scaled out but instead are usable on these smaller devices right from the moment the page loads.

To take advantage of this, we just add the following `<meta>` element to our page's `<head>`:

```
<meta name="viewport" content="width=device-width, »
  initial scale=1" />
```

The content attribute allows us to set up our parameters for the viewport. In this example, we first tell the browser that the default width of the viewport should be equal to the width of the device. In addition, the initial scale of the site should be 1, where each pixel is displayed 1 pixel wide.

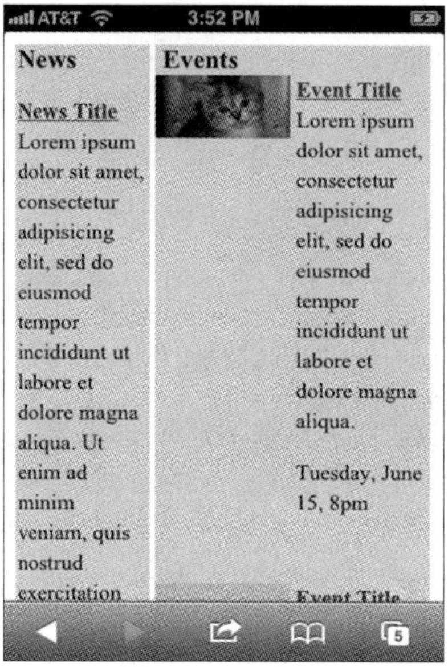

FIGURE 3.3
Once we set the <meta name="viewport"> element, the fluid site fits, snugly, on the phone.

If we wanted to, we could change the scale of our site, controlling just how zoomed out the page will look to users on a phone. In this example, I used the scale value of 1, which is equivalent to saying display pixels at 100 percent. If I wanted to display pixels at 50 percent of their normal size (that is, show two designed pixels for every physical pixel on the screen), I'd set the initial-scale attribute to .5. Depending on how your site works and how you expect your users to interact with it, you may want to change that initial scale. But remember, one of the frustrations smartphone owners have browsing the web is all the pinching and zooming they are expected to do just to interact with most websites. Make sure you have a compelling reason to change this initial scale from 1.

Now, if we add this viewport element to the HTML page we built in the last chapter, we can take advantage of the fluid layout and make the text on our site readable—almost (figure 3.3).

MEDIA TYPES

Besides different viewport sizes, web designers have always had to deal with many types of displays. In addition to screens, we must design for screen readers, which read out visual designs aloud for users with impaired vision; Braille devices, which turn our content into tactile feedback; standard and Braille printers; and a slew of handheld devices, like PDAs, that did not achieve the ubiquity of today's mobile devices. While most sites ignored these various device types, CSS gave designers a way to help optimize a visitor's experience on any device by serving up different CSS depending on the way the device "displayed" content. The media type gave designers nine kinds of display media to choose from.

This worked great for media types like screen and print, the two most popular types. Often designers would want their websites formatted differently when printed than when on the screen.[1] After all, navigation isn't needed on a printed page, so why display it? A site designer might use the print media type to hide the navigation on the printed version of a site:

```
@media screen {
    #navigation {
        display: block;
    }
}
@media print {
    #navigation {
        display: none;
    }
}
```


Over the past few years, we could have been serving up mobile-optimized CSS by using the handheld media type. But there were some problems with this approach. We've already seen one problem in the diversity of mobile device types available. Would a single "handheld" stylesheet make a good experience on an iPad, an Android phone, and a feature phone? Not likely. The different capabilities, not to mention screen sizes and resolutions, would replicate problems we've already encountered with our flexible layout.

There was a more practical reason that the handheld stylesheet couldn't solve our mobile problems: there weren't many of them when handheld devices started shipping with decent browsers. As such, the mobile browser developers looked to screen styles instead of handheld and resorted to viewport-scaling tricks to squeeze sites designed for desktop computers onto those small screens.

CSS MEDIA QUERIES

These limitations led to the release of media queries with CSS 3. Now you can test for a device's media type as well as the device's current "conditions": Is it in portrait or landscape? Current viewport width or height? Color density? A host of device conditions help us narrow down how best to represent the website on the users' device based on its current state.

Because many of the problems facing designers these days are the variety of screen sizes, it is no surprise that the most common media queries are for viewport width. Most of the conditions you can test for also allow you to specify the minimum and maximum values, rather than just a specific value, thus giving more flexibility to the stylesheet that is applied in different conditions. For instance, to change the `background-color` of a page to red if the viewport width is greater than 600 pixels, we could add this media query to our stylesheet:

```
@media screen and (min-width: 600px) {
     body {
          background-color: red;
     }
}
```


By simply adding the ability to test for current device conditions, media queries offer a powerful framework for tailoring our visual layouts to a variety of devices. Unlike device detection or browser sniffing, there is no need to update a library of specific devices. When a new device is released, it will simply load the appropriate flexible CSS using media queries and look great no matter the screen size. This allows us to serve layouts tailored for small or large screens, all with just CSS. Media queries let us build future-friendly layouts, ready to make our sites great for the next device that we haven't imagined yet.

Looking back to our fluid layout, we can start thinking about how to deal with the crowded columns when our viewport drops below 800 pixels. Since we've started with a layout designed for desktop-sized viewports (about 1000 pixels), we can add a query to change the visual layout of our columns to accommodate smaller screens. In our last example, our left column was narrow in our mockup, and in our fixed grid turned out to be around 32 percent of the width of the container. Our problem at smaller viewport sizes below 650 pixels is that the actual width of this column drops to a maximum of 208 pixels (32 percent of 650 pixels). This is simply not wide enough to comfortably handle the content.

So we can tell the browser to change the CSS at viewports under 650 pixels to better accommodate this change. A possible solution is to change the number of grid columns each content column occupies, making the narrow left column wider. If `.left and .right` each occupied six columns, then `.left` would get more room to spread out. We might have to move the event text below the images to keep the event content from seeming crowded, but it makes the news items feel readable again (figure 3.4).

Calculating these new proportional widths can be done with our old fixed-width grid we used for reference earlier. Since proportions are the same no matter the

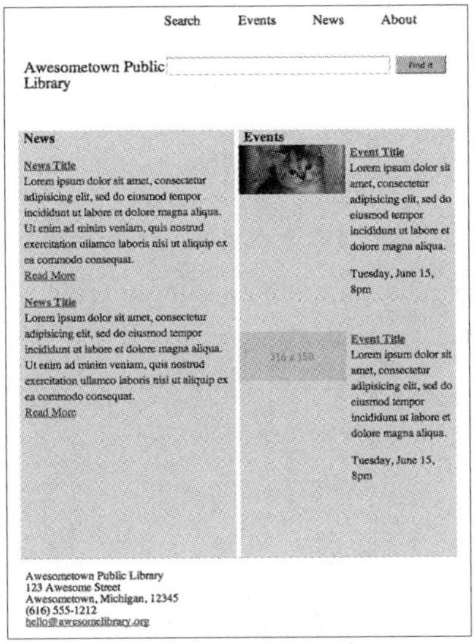

FIGURE 3.4
We can split the width of our columns, making them more equal.

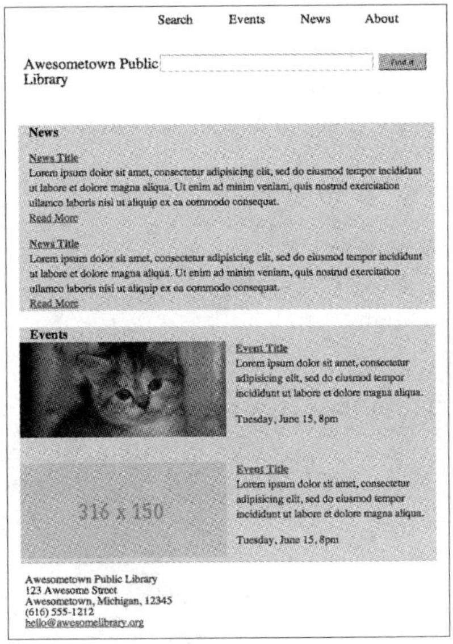

FIGURE 3.5
Another choice might be to remove the floats, stacking the content top to bottom.

container size, any time you need to know a context for calculating relative sizes, go back to your fixed grid. Our fixed grid was contained in the 964 pixel wide `#page`, and each content column will be six grid columns and five grid gutters wide. Since each grid column was 73 pixels with 8-pixel gutters, we can do a little simple math to get the widths of our new columns:

$$(73 \times 6) + (8 \times 5) = 478 \text{ pixels}$$

To calculate the proportional width, we go back to our `Target ÷ Context = Result` formula:

$$478 \div 964 = 49.585062240664\%$$

Now we can change our layout with the following media query:

```
@media screen and (max-width: 650px) {
    .left,
    .right {
        width: 49.585062240664%;
```

```
    }
    .right .event-img,
    .right .event {
        float: none;
    }
} /* end media query */
```

Since our earlier style for `.left` and `.right` included the floats, we need only to change the width, since the media query will retain the previous styles.

Another solution is to change our visual layout to stop floating the two columns and instead create a single-column layout (figure 3.5):

```
@media screen and (max-width: 650px) {
.left,
.right {
    float: none;
    width: 100%;
    }
}
```


In the same way that we can adapt the layout for smaller screens, we can accommodate larger screens. Once the viewport gets beyond 1200 pixels, the line lengths in the right column become difficult to read. Some constraint might be needed above a certain threshold. Here we can switch from a fluid layout to fixed width layout centered on the page (figure 3.6):

```
@media screen and (min-width: 1200px) {
    #page {
        background-color: #fff;
        margin: 0 auto; /* center the content */
        width: 68.75em; /* 16 / 1100px = 68.75em */
    }
    body {
        background-color: #eee;
        /* Show area not in container */
    }
}
```

Locking a screen layout into a centered, fixed-width might not be our best option, either. If we had more content below our left and right columns, we might

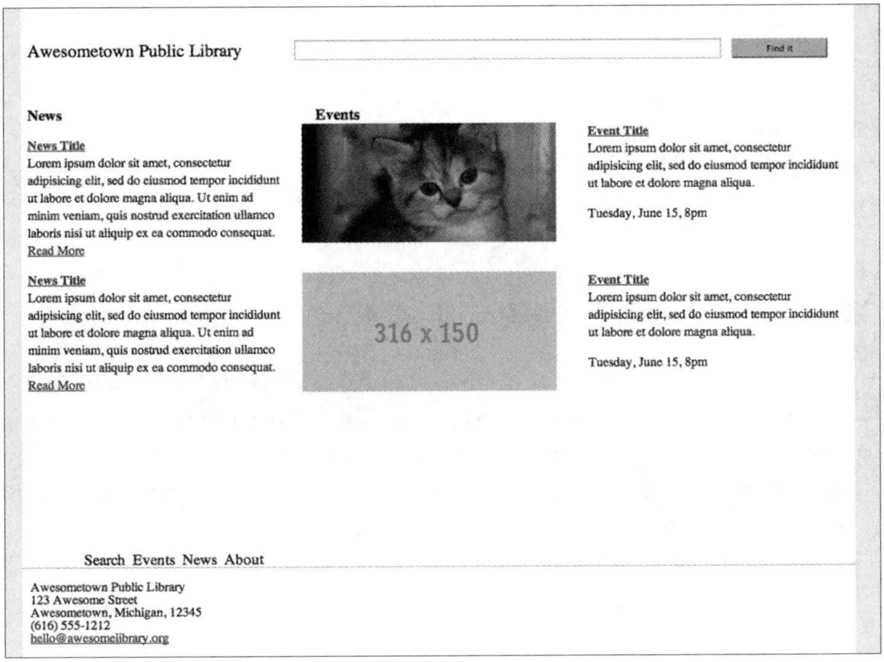

FIGURE 3.6
Constraining the width of our content on large screens might be a good idea.

change our visual layout to three or four columns for viewports wider than 1200 pixels. How you adapt your layout to accommodate different viewports depends on your content as well as your audience.

VALUES IN MEDIA QUERIES

In the previous chapter we worked hard to build a fluid layout that not only would scale and adapt to changes in the viewport but also would scale and zoom according to the preferences of our users. By sizing text with ems, we avoided locking fonts and vertical heights into a pixel-based framework. We can do the same for our media queries. Instead of tying our queries to pixel values, which do not change with user preferences, we should use relative measurements so our media queries work appropriately with our users' needs. So instead of the two earlier media queries using pixel values, we would use the following:

```
@media screen and (max-width: 40em) {
    /* 640 ÷ 16 = 40 */
}
@media screen and (min-width: 75em) {
    /* 1200 ÷ 16 = 75 */
}
```

OTHER CONDITIONS TO TEST FOR

The example media queries I've shown so far have all been for the size of the viewport, and these are the most common media queries to use for responsive designs. But there are many other device conditions you can test for. Currently, all the conditions relate to the visual aspects of the display because media queries were designed to address the limitations of media types for visual displays. If you want to test for more than one condition, you can chain multiple queries with the Boolean "and" operator.

device-width and device-height—measures screen size, not viewport

orientation—portrait or landscape?

aspect ratio—measures the viewport

device aspect ratio—measures the device screen

color—measured in bits

color index—number of colors

Monochrome—measured in bits

resolution—measured in dots per inch (dpi)

scan—progressive or scan

grid—feature phone grid-based display

You may never need to use any media queries besides width and height. By understanding your site's content and your users' needs, you can decide which conditions to test for and how your site will adapt.

DETERMINING BREAK POINTS

A break point is the point at which you need a media query to load a new set of styles to change the visual layout of your site. There is a school of thought that you should marry break points to common device widths, so that you have a set of styles for 320 pixels for older iPhones and Androids in portrait, one at 480 pixels for phones in landscape, one at 600 pixels for seven-inch tablets like the Kindle Fire, one at 768 pixels for the iPad in portrait, and finally, a 1024-pixel layout for iPads in landscape and desktop computers. But this makes sense only if you ignore the multitude of devices on the market today and are blind to the fact that new devices with different resolutions and dimensions will be released every day on into the future. In fact, this mentality isn't much different from the old "consensual hallucination" that we could predict the size at which users would view our site. A better strategy for determining break points is to match them to your content.

In the previous example, we started with our content and then changed the viewport until the layout "broke." That's where we needed to put in a break point. It had nothing to do with the device's screen width and everything to do with the structure of our content. To fill out the website, we simply need to test the visual layout of the site at all possible viewport widths, from large to small. When the layout breaks, add a break point and adjust the styles. You don't need to worry whether your site will look great on new devices with large or impossibly small screens, because you've already tested those sizes when you were determining break points for your layout.

NOTE

1. A decade ago, in my first web design job, my boss reviewed every page I designed by looking at a printed copy and insisted that web sites be treated like books. After a few weeks of frustration, I took to doing one design for screen and another for print. The print version would accommodate everything my boss wanted while the screen version finally allowed the site to take advantage of the web's unique nature (or at least I thought so). My boss never knew I was making two versions of the site, and everyone was happy.

Chapter Four

Performance

When Ethan Marcotte first introduced responsive design in 2010, he focused on techniques for adapting the layout of sites onto different screens.[1] While this is crucial to adapting to different devices, we must also consider how all of these flexible, fluid assets—our stylesheets, JavaScript, images, and other media—are loaded. For just as an inflexible layout can break the visual layout of a site on a small screen, loading too many kilobytes (kb) over a slow connection has the same effect: it makes the site unusable on a particular device.

In 2008 the average website was 312 kb. Today, it's more than 1400, more than a megabyte (Mb), and growing.[2] The average number of requests—when the user's browser asks to download a stylesheet, script, or image—have increased, too, from fifty in 2008 to eighty-eight in 2012.[3] We're sending more kilobytes over more server requests than ever before. Of course, the web is a rich place for all of these assets: gorgeous, high-resolution images; interactive scripts that turn websites into fully functional applications; and videos of cats who love vacuum cleaners.[4]

This richness is part of what makes the web so indispensable, but it also can be a source of frustration for our users if we aren't doing everything we can to make sure all of these extra assets are necessary and optimized. In libraries, we often don't know the true weight of our web pages, because they are written and hosted by a vendor or are a mishmash of embedded content we've pulled from a number of systems. But this neglect has a price, because our patrons notice poor performance.

In 2006, Google, already the dominant search engine, tried an experiment. Users had been asking for more results per page for years, and so they tried making the default number of results thirty rather than ten. They ran some tests with users, and saw traffic (and revenue) drop by 20 percent when users got thirty results instead of ten. It wasn't the added results that caused the problem. Rather, it was something the team hadn't controlled for: performance. A ten-result page took .4 seconds to load, whereas thirty results took half a second longer, .9 seconds. That extra half second caused one-fifth of users to leave.[5]

But it's not just folks on desktop computers who expect speed. In chapter 1, I cited a study by Compuware that showed that 71 percent of mobile web users expect sites to be as fast or faster on their phones than on desktop computers. Sixty percent won't wait more than three seconds for a page to load, and a third won't come back if they have an initial slow experience with a site on their phone.[6]

We rarely take these performance expectations into consideration when building a new library site or evaluating a vendor tool. In fact, like the mythical screen size our users shared, we are under a collective hallucination that everyone has a fast broadband connection at all times. But we have no guarantee that patrons who visit our sites are on broadband or dial-up, 4G, or something slower like EDGE. Just as we can't make assumptions about our users' devices or screens, we can't assume our bloated websites will stream down fast connections to all of our users. To be truly responsive, then, we must consider how well our sites perform on different devices, not just how they look.

When we looked at media queries, we saw that beginning with the smallest screen can help us focus the elements of our layout to find what is really important. Once we have the design elements for small screens in place, then we can enhance the layout with size. The same strategy can apply to designing sites for performance. We need to design our sites to perform well on slow connections and then enhance them where necessary based on what we can tell about the user's device and connection.

Because all of our performance problems stem from sending too many bytes over too many connections, there are two ways to improve our site's performance: send fewer bytes over fewer connections.

CONCATENATING FILES

The value of sending fewer bytes is immediately apparent. Sending fewer bytes means that our sites will load faster, not having to wait as long for all assets to load. As we've seen, that makes users happy, even at the expense of features they think they want. YouTube experimented with streamlining its player a few years ago, replacing the bloated 1.2 Mb Flash player with a lightweight, 98 kb HTML5 player. Chris Zacharias, the engineer who wrote the streamlined code, expected to see a huge drop in page-load times with the 1 Mb drop in page weight. He was shocked to see that load time *increased*.

What he discovered was that one variable had not been controlled for: geography. Huge areas of the world that were underserved by broadband Internet were now able to use YouTube for the first time, since the player wasn't so heavy.[7] The new player would actually load over slow connections, allowing new users to stream video.

Most libraries do not serve an international population, but there are still plenty of folks we do serve who can access the web only over slow connections, either dial-up or EDGE on a mobile device. These data connections are not free. Every byte we send a patron over a cellular connection costs money. And frankly, loading a bloated 1.2 Mb site over 3G isn't exactly speedy. And if you can reduce the load time for users on slow connections, those same benefits will trickle up the chain, making your site that much faster and more responsive to users who do have broadband or another fast connection.

There are two simple techniques that can help reduce the size of your web pages: compress your files or don't send them in the first place. There are more sophisticated techniques that involve tinkering with your servers, but these simple tasks will make the most immediate difference.

If you are using embedded social media buttons or JavaScript libraries like jQuery, ask yourself whether your users really benefit from those assets in relation to the trade-offs in performance that come from using them. Social media sharing buttons, like the ones in figure 4.1, load an image as well as several JavaScript files to track usage and give you up-to-date counts on how many folks have "liked" or "tweeted" your page.

The example in figure 4.1 uses six server requests for almost 50 kb of data. But using just an image linked to your Twitter account, like figure 4.2, uses only one request for about 2 kb. If you think your users are fine with loading an extra 47 kb on your site to know how many other people have tweeted about your library, then go ahead with the most complex button. But in this case, the extra overhead simply isn't worth it.

Likewise, using JavaScript libraries like jQuery makes it really easy to build interactive sites quickly, with great cross-browser support. But that ease in writing code comes at a cost. Scripts now account for more than 200 kb of the average

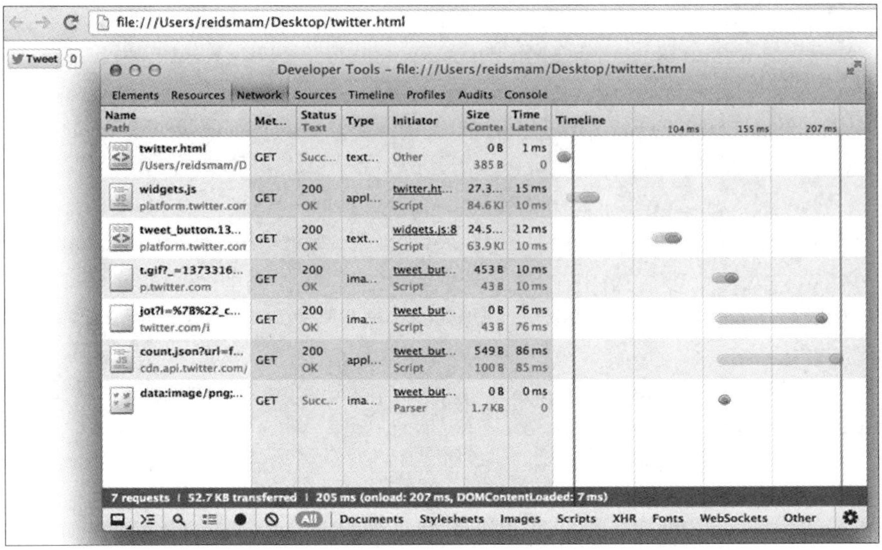

FIGURE 4.1
This social media button weighs a lot.

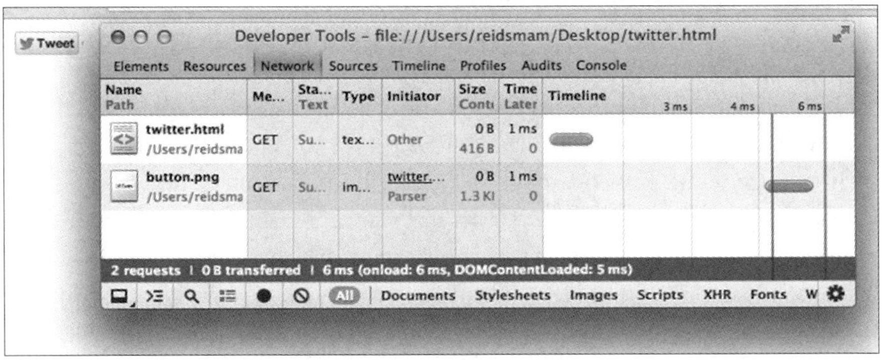

FIGURE 4.2
This social media button doesn't weigh a lot.

web page.[8] Loading the current unminimized version of jQuery goes beyond that, weighing in at 280 kb. And that's just the library—this doesn't include your code!

Minimizing the script with a JavaScript compressor can knock the library down to 90 kb, and setting up your server to send "gzipped" files or using Google's developer Content Delivery Network (CDN)[9] will take it down further, to 33 kb. But if you are using jQuery to power a few accordions to hide content or a slideshow, these tools could just as easily be written in JavaScript, which does not require you to load the extra library. Rather than burden your users with another asset to download, we can write simple scripts more carefully and remove this dependency.

Of course, some times the trade-off is worth it. Often when I am working on improving vendor sites, I don't have the ability to change the code the vendor uses to display the site or to control user interactions. A lot of software for libraries is crummy, designed to fit around database structures or the way librarians think rather than catering to patron use. Powerful JavaScript libraries like jQuery can be invaluable here in helping you better control the experience for your patrons. I'll talk more about this in chapter 9, but there are times when loading an extra library will help you improve the patron experience so much that it is worth the extra overhead.

If you're certain that you need to load the scripts or styles you have, then reducing the size of the files can also save some bytes. Stylesheets often have a lot of white space to help make them more readable by humans. But computers don't need white space, even though it takes up bytes in a CSS file to represent it. A stylesheet compressor like that at http://csscompressor.com can strip out all of this white space and reduce the size of your stylesheet.

JavaScript files have more opportunity for file-size reduction. An online tool like http://jscompress.com can not only strip out white space but also simplify your variable names and syntax. It's not unusual to have a minimized JavaScript file weigh just a third or less of its uncompressed parent, as we saw with loading a minimized version of jQuery earlier. With scripts taking up more and more of the average web page's weight these days, minimization is a great and easy way to improve your site's performance.

It might not make intuitive sense that sending all of your styles, for instance, in three or four files will be slower than sending them all in one file, since the same number of bytes are being sent. But more happens in a server request than just loading files. First, the browser must make a connection to find the host server wherever it lives on the web (DNS). Once the server is found, then the browser requests the file. The server receives the request, but it takes a bit of time between the request and when it starts sending the requested file. This time is called "time till first byte," or TTFB. Finally, the file we requested is sent. If there are two files requested, then the process starts over again from the request if the second file is on the same server, and after TTFB, the second file comes through (figure 4.3).

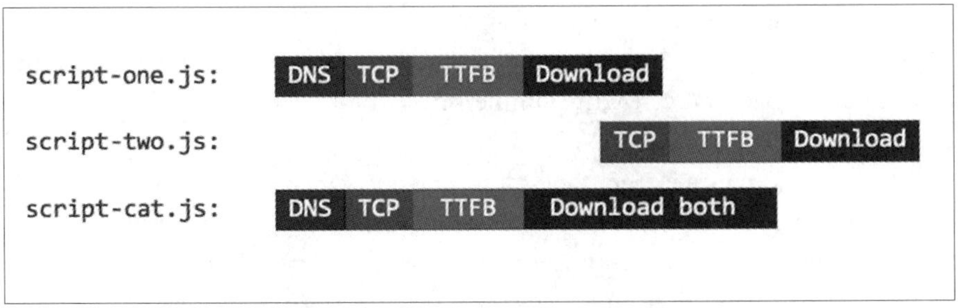

FIGURE 4.3
Loading one file over several saves time.

If we sent all of that data in one file instead of two, we would cut out the time needed for the second request, as well as the TTFB. We'd still send the same number of bytes after our DNS request, but by reducing the number of files we've requested, we are able to load things a little faster. When you think about concatenating scripts and stylesheets across an average site with eighty-eight requests, we could drastically reduce loading time.

Compression isn't just for CSS and JavaScript. You can also compress HTML. If you can't make changes to your server, stripping comments and white space with an online compression tool like that at http://htmlcompressor.com can help you serve smaller HTML files.

But simply minimizing and concatenating our stylesheets, scripts, and HTML won't make our sites perform optimally. More than 850 kb, or 61 percent, of the average web page comes from images.[10] By optimizing our images and media, we can really improve our site's performance.

OPTIMIZING IMAGES AND MEDIA

Image and video files are large, and that shows in the disproportionate amount of the average web page they take up. To make high-quality images, the files need to remain large; otherwise, our images will start to degrade and look pixelly. But an image that needs to look sharp on a 1200-pixel-wide monitor will be unnecessarily large for a smartphone. If we were worried about sending unnecessary bytes by leaving white space in our stylesheets and scripts, that is small potatoes compared to what we can save with careful image optimization.

Jason Griggsby experimented with the images Ethan Marcotte used in his original article on responsive web design.[11] When Marcotte demonstrated using the CSS property `max-width: 100%;` to allow images to comfortably scale across devices, Griggsby noticed that a lot of the information contained in the image file was going to waste, since the smaller device could display the image only at a smaller size. The phone, however, still downloads the full image.

The original demonstration page Marcotte created used six images, each 330 × 345 pixels. The images were between 26 and 44 kb in size, with most weighing in at about 35 kb. All together, the six images were 208.3 kb. If they were loaded on an iPhone, the images would be displayed only at 150 × 157 pixels. If the images were left as is, the iPhone would download all 200-plus kilobytes of the images and scale the images to fit the smaller viewport. However, Griggsby resized the images to the target size for the phone, 150 × 157 pixels, and then reran the download to see what the savings was. Each resized image was around 6 or 8 kb, rather than an average of 35 kb. All together, the six images were just under 46 kb. That's a 78 percent savings in file size if the images are scaled for the appropriate screen size, as opposed to letting the browser scale the larger, original images. As Griggsby says, "Downloading 160K unnecessarily on a mobile device is nothing to sneeze at no matter how good the mobile phone is."

Of course, resizing every image to match a target viewport defeats the purpose of fluid images and would put us right back into the reactionary mindset of designing for the devices that exist today. So how can we load the appropriate images for the device, and perhaps for the connection? After all, as YouTube learned, not everyone with a desktop computer has a broadband connection, so we can't necessarily guarantee that a larger screen means a fast connection.

With CSS background images, we can use media queries to control which images show up, but browsers are a bit inconsistent about how these images are handled[12] Using media queries to toggle between different background images depending on device conditions is fairly consistent, but some pretty common mobile browsers, specifically the default browser in early versions of Android, will load all of the images specified in the stylesheet, whether or not they are relevant to the existing media query. While this would be the ideal solution for background images, instead of having users of older Android phones downloading one large image, they'd be downloading a large image *and* a smaller image. So this isn't much of a solution.

Even worse is simply using a `display:none` override in certain media queries to either show or not show background images or even images in an `<img>` tag. In that case, virtually all browsers will download the image, whether or not the media query is active.

The only reliable way to handle background images with media queries is to hide their parent elements, but this solution isn't remotely how we expect HTML and CSS to work together, so I don't think it's much of a solution. Besides, none of these CSS media query tricks will help us with regular <img> elements, arguably the most common types of images we're dealing with in our sites.

There isn't an easy solution for loading the appropriate media assets depending on device conditions right now. But there is hope. HTML5 introduced the <video> element, which is media-aware. You can specify different video source files to be loaded depending on device conditions, and the browsers all understand to load only the appropriate video. The following HTML shows how a low- and high-resolution video might be specified for a responsive site that didn't want to force users to download the significantly larger high-resolution video if their devices could not take advantage of the extra resolution:


```
<video controls="controls">
    <source src="lores.mp4" type="video/mp4" »
      media="screen and (max-width: 48em)">
    <source src="highres.mp4" type="video/mp4">
</video>
```

What we need is a media-savvy element for images like the <video> element, and there are several proposals on the table, including a <picture> element that would behave like the HTML5 <video> element. For more information on how these proposals are coming along, follow the work of the Responsive Images Community Group at the W3C (www.w3.org/community/respimg).

In the meantime, there are some things we can do now to make our images perform better with our current sites, and many of these techniques are adaptations of what we have seen earlier: send fewer bytes over fewer connections. If the image is essential to users' experience, then you can at least make the image load faster for your site's users.

The easiest way to send fewer bytes is to optimize our images to find the best balance between quality and file size. Although saving an image in Photoshop gives you the ability to specify the "quality" of an image when you save it, these images often contain a lot of additional information that does not need to be there. Using a program designed to optimize images, like ImageOptim on the Mac, can cut the file sizes on your images by 25 to 40 percent in many cases.

But you can also cut down on the number of requests your site makes for images, especially small icons or logos, by making an image sprite. Basically, a sprite is one large image that contains many smaller images tiled within it. You then load the image sprite wherever you need one of the images and specify how the sprite will be positioned so that the user sees only the icon needed. This has the benefit of only doing one request to get many images.

You can also use an icon font like Symbolset to handle your icons instead of images.[13] Icon fonts have the benefit of very low file size, and they combine many icons into a single request. By using an icon font, browsers that cannot load web fonts might have an accessible fallback, as well, since the icons are sometimes translated from the words they represent.

If you're really eager to cut down on server requests, you can also encode your images in base64 and include them inline in your HTML document. Images are, after all, just a bunch of bits the computer translates into visual images, so including them right in your HTML isn't a problem for the browser. The `<img>` element here shows a base64 encoded image of a pencil icon:


```
<img alt="" src="data:image/png;base64,iVBORw0KGgoAAA
ANSUhEUgAAACAAAAAfCAYAAACGVs+MAAABxUlEQVR42u3Xz0vTcRzHcadMX
ak0PeWpungU/QvEv6Bjgtm00DrG2GIsZZgmaSESIl12iEBiuM1t2g9/dEiI
ebL+gxDUozKn6cFPz8Pr8P0DfH+9+IIHe99e743vj89qnHNX6noBX0pIAA
1XsgBpRRG/0e3rAqQea3Cyiy5fFiBhtCMG5/EXnaYLkFv4gR204TmcR95s
AdKC73BSRhhROFxgyGQB0oxvOMRLVFXBQ+xqdIJpDXHUXfpC5AbKOAYA5
5vPoXXmqMmT0KV51HFI8/F9wYTmuMmj2ISQhYniOCrCmcwrjlh8i4gjcj
gFINYVeE7pDQnTV5GpAGf8Q9DKKlwFmOax0zehqQeizjDYxRUOIdRzSmT1
7HKP+EcT5BT4XskNb8yOQ+QID6qfBhLKpxHQvOkyYFEt1oapxhBRoULeKF5
yuxERJ6pZB8bmj8gpnna7EhGenEXWThZRlTzW7MzIQmgjBLCKnY4wAVmTQ+
l5A4qKsloiaLntgtYL/AAziOHe3iKWtNjOQngPv6ovIpt9Pjyv4C04Sf6E
EEH9JP7s0AIt6//mvnhP/yTigYztZTLAAAAAElFTkSuQmCC" />
```


Unfortunately, older versions of Internet Explorer do not support base64 images, so make sure you use descriptive `alt` tags.

If you feel comfortable with JavaScript and are willing to experiment, there are several ways to get responsive images today without waiting for the W3C to approve a particular format like `<picture>`.

One of the earliest solutions is Scott Jehl's Picturefill.[14] Using JavaScript, Picturefill takes a group of spans marked up with data attributes and allows you to use the proposed `<picture>` element syntax today. You can specify different images to load depending on various media queries. If you had three different versions of an image you wanted to load depending on screen width, you might mark up your Picturefill HTML like this:

```
<span data-picture data-alt="Students using new group study
  rooms">
    <span data-src="small.jpg"></span>
    <span data-src="medium.jpg" »
      data-media="(min-width: 400px)"></span>
    <span data-src="large.jpg" »
      data-media="(min-width: 800px)"></span>
    <span data-src="extralarge.jpg" »
      data-media="(min-width: 1000px)"></span>
    <noscript>
        <img src="external/imgs/small.jpg" »
          alt="Students using new group study rooms">
    </noscript>
</span>
```


The script would then look for the various data attributes on the `<span>`s and load the appropriate image. For browsers without JavaScript support, Jehl proposes using the `<noscript>` element to force loading of a static image.

This is a great solution for loading the appropriate images for certain device conditions, but it does have some drawbacks. If the browser does not support media queries, then the script alone will not add support for that. There are still a few popular browsers, like Internet Explorer 7 and 8, that do not support media queries, and so Jehl's solution will not work for users of those browsers.

I'll talk more in the next chapter about how to get around lack of media query support in older versions of Internet Explorer, but if your user base is Internet Explorer heavy, you might want to consider a different solution to serve responsive images today.

Fortunately, Chris Coyier and Christopher Schmitt have created a nice matrix of techniques for serving up responsive images.[15] There are a lot of factors that might go into your decision to serve up responsive images, so this tool can be invaluable for helping you find the best solution today.

Of course, your site might not be image heavy. If you don't have a lot of images, especially large ones, you might be able to get away with some of the techniques above for optimizing the images you do have. Whatever you do, remember that our patrons expect our sites to load quickly, so take this into account when you are creating new content. Will it load quickly? Is it necessary for the patron to complete their task or learn about this service? Is it worth the time and bandwidth it will take to download? These questions will help guide you to the best solution for your library's website.

NOTES

1. Ethan Marcotte, "Responsive Web Design," May 25, 2010, http://alistapart.com/articles/responsive-web-design.
2. HTTP Archive, "Interesting Stats," http://httparchive.org/interesting.php.
3. Website Optimization, "Average Web Page Size Triples since 2008," November 11, 2012, http://websiteoptimization.com/speed/tweak/average-web-page; HTTP Archive, "Trends," http://httparchive.org/trends.php?s=All&minlabel=Nov+15+2010&maxlabel=Apr+1+2013&bytesTotal&reqTotal.
4. My favorite is "Cat Really Loves Being Vacuumed," YouTube video, 2:59, posted by Krzysztof Smejlis, November 5, 2012, www.youtube.com/watch?v=FTRhiOeRzfA.
5. Greg Linden, "Marissa Mayer at Web 2.0," November 9, 2006, http://glinden.blogspot.com/2006/11/marissa-mayer-at-web-20.html.
6. Compuware, "New Study Reveals the Mobile Web Disappoints Global Customers," July 19, 2011, http://www.compuware.com/en_us/about/press-releases/2011/7/new-study-reveals-the-mobile-web-disappoints-global-consumers.html.
7. Chris Zacharias, "Page Weight Matters," http://blog.chriszacharias.com/page-weight-matters.
8. HTTP Archive, "Interesting Stats," http://httparchive.org/interesting.
9. Google has better servers than you do. You can load jQuery from its servers, which increases the likelihood that the file will already be cached on your patron's machine. If it's not, Google's servers are plenty fast. Learn more at "Google Hosted Libraries—Developer's Guide," at https://developers.google.com/speed/libraries/devguide.
10. HTTP Archive, "Interesting Stats," http://httparchive.org/interesting.php.
11. Jason Grigsby, "CSS Media Query for Mobile Is Fool's Gold," August 3, 2010, http://blog.cloudfour.com/css-media-query-for-mobile-is-fools-gold/.
12. Tim Kadlec, "Media Query & Asset Downloading Results," April 10, 2012, http://timkadlec.com/2012/04/media-query-asset-downloading-results/.
13. Symbolset, http://symbolset.com.
14. Scott Jehl, "Picturefill," GitHub, https://github.com/scottjehl/picturefill.
15. Chris Coyier, "Which Responsive Images Solution Should You Use?" May 11, 2012, http://css-tricks.com/which-responsive-images-solution-should-you-use/.

Chapter Five

Responsive Web Design and Support

Since media queries are a relatively new addition to CSS, they are not supported in every browser. While most current browsers have robust media query support, Internet Explorer version 8 and earlier, for instance, do not understand media queries. Since these browsers are still heavily used (probably even at your library), we have to find a way to help Internet Explorer users get the most out of our sites if we rely on media queries to deliver styles based on device conditions.

The problem is, because Internet Explorer 8 and below do not understand media queries, they just ignore them. This has the benefit of not crashing the browser, but all of those styles we worked hard to create for different device conditions are then ignored by a whole group of people using an old browser.

MOBILE FIRST VERSUS DESKTOP FIRST

A browser not understanding media queries isn't necessarily a bad thing. Bryan Riger, writing about the issue of older versions of Internet Explorer, said it best: "the absence of support for media queries is in fact the first media query."[1] If a media query is nothing but a test to see if the device meets certain criteria, then whether or not that device supports these tests is just as important as a test for screen width or color depth.

This makes it important to choose exactly how we are going to create our "base" styles, that is, those that are not inside of media queries. There are basically two ways to approach this: desktop first or mobile first. If we design for the desktop first, then we put all of the styles for the desktop site in our CSS without media queries, and then use `max-width` media queries to overwrite the desktop styles to adapt the site to smaller screens. Browsers like Internet Explorer 8 and below will simply load the styles not in media queries—the desktop styles—and the site will look as expected. This can be a good solution if you have a lot of users still on older versions of Internet Explorer.

The downside of this solution is that it assumes that users are coming to your site on large screens, and so requires devices with smaller screens to support media queries in order to give them an experience tailored for their smaller viewports. As we saw in an earlier chapter, half of Americans who visited library websites in 2012 tried at least once on a mobile device. And as smartphone adoption continues to expand, those numbers will likely grow.

Of course, this doesn't automatically mean that your site will be more useful to folks using Internet Explorer because it takes advantage of the screen real estate. The usefulness of your site might have nothing to do with layout, and everything to do with the content you are offering. As Bruce Lawson said in a recent article for *Smashing* magazine, "The reason many 'full websites' are unusable on mobile phones is because many full websites are unusable on any device."[2]

As libraries, we are especially prone to this problem. Our mission is to provide the right information for our users when they need it, and so we tend to shy away from trimming content, because somewhere, someone might need that page, or paragraph, or link. This is the legacy of Ranganathan's rule, "Every book a reader." We start with the implicit assumption that every bit of content has a patron, somewhere, who needs it, and our mission is to be the conduit to connect that person to what he or she needs.

The problem with this mentality is that it adds to the difficulty in using the library for everyone. If we make all of our patrons sift through rarely used content to access more commonly used materials, then we're not serving anyone well. Information is no longer scarce, and folks go to a thousand other places for it before they think of coming to the library website. We'll serve our users better by offering a more curated and streamlined approach to connecting them with information. That might mean cutting out tools that librarians like to use but that don't serve users well. By knowing why you have a website and making sure the content supports your site's goals, then you'll serve your patrons better.

Designing your library mobile site first is a great way to think through the content you have and what is important to your patrons. If we're reluctant to fill up the limited screen space on a small screen with the same content we see on the desktop site on the grounds that it will clutter up the "mobile" experience, then what makes us think those features are necessary for patrons coming to our site with large screens?

If we don't want to make assumptions about the kinds of devices our users have, it would be best to start with a layout that does not make any assumptions about screen size: a simple, linear layout. If we think of layout as an enhancement, then this approach makes sense. The web is fluid, and our patrons come to the library website for the content, not for the design or layout. By setting an appropriate baseline for how our site should look and work for all users, we can then enhance the site, improving from the baseline depending on the patron's device conditions.

Starting from a small screen view helps us do just that. We start with basic typographic styles, add in styles for color and form (e.g., padding, margins), and by default our site will be rendered linearly, since our chunks of content will be rendered as block elements. We then use min-width media queries to adjust the layout of those various content chunks, and perhaps to adjust typography and color, as the device becomes more capable of handling a larger canvas. Rather than starting from the most enhanced version, designed for wide screens with lots of content, we start with the most basic version of our site we're comfortable serving users. Everyone gets at least an acceptable, minimal experience. If your browser is more capable, or if your device meets certain conditions, then you'll get an enhanced experience. We build the site up to meet our patrons' capabilities rather than strip away features that cannot be used.

INTERNET EXPLORER–CONDITIONAL COMMENTS

Of course, starting from mobile first means that older browsers, like Internet Explorer 8 and below, will ignore styles that enhance our layout for larger screens. Users on Internet Explorer will get your site served in a linear layout, stretched to fill the viewport. If the window is full-screen or close, this could be a crummy looking site (figure 5.1). This is not ideal, although your site is still usable. But if you are a library, there is a good chance you have a lot of visits from folks on older versions of Internet Explorer. People with older PCs at home who are not tech-savvy enough to download a new browser like Firefox or Chrome, and conservative or underfunded information technology departments, often hold on to legacy browsers that do not support media queries.

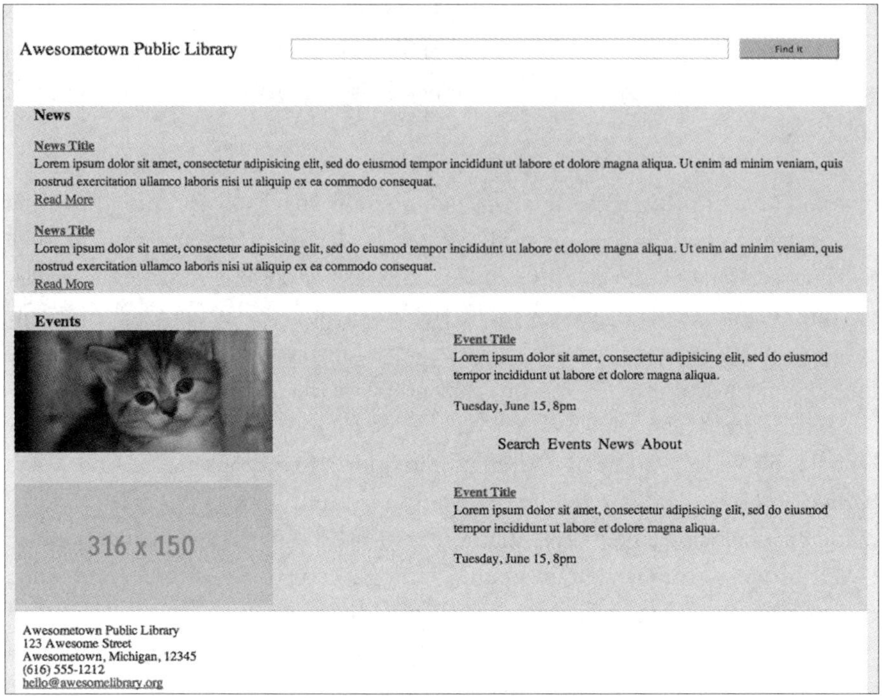

FIGURE 5.1
Oh, that looks terrible.

There is an easy way to serve a desktop layout to IE while still serving a mobile-first layout to all other devices. Your site will not have the flexibility of a fully responsive site, although you can certainly make it fluid so it can still adapt to changes in the viewport. But by using conditional comments aimed only at Internet Explorer, you can serve up desktop-style layouts despite Internet Explorer's not understanding media queries.

Internet Explorer–conditional comments have been around for a long time. They allow you to do a simple test that checks whether the browser loading the site is Internet Explorer. If the test shows Internet Explorer, then it will load whatever markup falls between the opening and closing comments. What we can do is create a stylesheet that loads all of the styles inside our media queries for Internet Explorer 8 and below:

```
<!--[if lt IE 9]>
    <link rel="stylesheet" href="css/iestyles.css" />
<![endif]-->
```

By loading these styles after our stylesheet with the rest of the media queries, Internet Explorer will load all the styles needed to give us the appropriate layout for wide screens.

To make our lives a little easier in an earlier chapter, we also took advantage of a CSS rule that let us change the box model to make it easier to calculate padding and borders. Unfortunately, Internet Explorer 8 and below do not understand the CSS `box-sizing` rule. If you've chosen that route and have a number of folks still using legacy browsers, you might want to make some adjustments to the calculated padding of your elements so that your layout doesn't cause problems on older browsers.

The downside of this approach is that you are making patrons with older versions of Internet Explorer download more assets than other browsers, since they will download all of the unused media queries as well as the Internet Explorer–specific stylesheets. Depending on the size of your stylesheets, this can be a burden. You'll have to weigh the benefits of sending extra bytes to some users to determine whether the trade-offs are worth it.

JAVASCRIPT SOLUTIONS

Another option is to patch media query support in unsupported browsers with JavaScript. Scott Jehl, the creator of Picturefill, has also written a small JavaScript library that adds media query support in Internet Explorer 8 and below if JavaScript is available, called Respond.js (http://github.com/scottjehl/Respond). Weighing in at less than 1 kb, it is extremely small and so does not add a significant performance burden. Respond.js lets Internet Explorer users see your site resize as they change the viewport, so the experience is much like what users experience in browsers that support media queries natively.

Respond.js works best when you are only loading a single stylesheet, and needs to be loaded after all of your CSS. Since a lot of library systems break up CSS into several files, or require the use of `@import` rules to add additional styles, Respond.js won't always be an option. At Grand Valley State University, my library website uses a slightly modified version of the campus template. Unfortunately, the template uses seven stylesheets, and Respond.js can't parse through all of our sheets.

Other JavaScript solutions to patch media query support exist that allow for multiple stylesheets, but they come with their own caveats. Some require nonstandard syntax, such as adding specific comments to your media queries so they will be parsed. Libraries like cssmediaqueries.js let you use standard media query syntax like respond.js and parse multiple stylesheets, but minimized weigh more than 15 kb.[3]

Ultimately, you'll need to decide which approach fits your patrons and your site best. In the next half of the book, I'll walk you through converting an existing fixed-width site to be responsive and show how many of these ideals we've discussed sometimes won't make sense for our real-world applications. Hopefully that will help you make sense of how best to serve your patrons and all of their devices.

NOTES

1. Yiibu, "Rethinking the Mobile Web," September 10, 2010, www.slideshare.net/bryanrieger/rethinking-the-mobile-web-by-yiibu.
2. Bruce Lawson, "Why We Shouldn't Make Separate Mobile Websites," April 19, 2012, www.smashingmagazine.com/2012/04/19/why-we-shouldnt-make-separate-mobile-websites/.
3. Wouter van der Graaf, "CSS3-Mediaqueries.js," http://code.google.com/p/css3-mediaqueries-js/.

Chapter Six

Going Responsive: First Steps

Once you understand the basics of responsive design, it's time to start thinking about how to make your existing site responsive. This is usually the time in libraries when we form a committee and then spend the next year fighting about what should be included on the new "redesigned" library website. But we don't need to go this route to make our sites more usable. There is a better way.

Library website redesigns are a political minefield. Because the website serves different purposes for different library stakeholders, there are often conflicting goals and requirements that must be addressed when a full-site redesign is proposed. That's why I recommend that you never redesign your library website. Instead, make small, iterative changes based on user and stakeholder testing, and within a few months, you might find that you've redesigned your website in baby steps without ever convening a committee.[1]

But there are more practical reasons to avoid a redesign just to make your site responsive. Libraries often don't have the in-house expertise to work on complex design solutions, or if they do, the person responsible often can't focus on the website full-time. I have a colleague I know who is the systems, web services, and liaison librarian to five departments. She works the same number of hours I do. She has skills, but not time.

All of the books on the market today about responsive web design walk you through creating a new project from scratch. And there are good reasons for this, many of which we've covered in the first half of this book. But in libraries, this kind of start-from-scratch rethinking of our websites is often not possible. But you don't need to redesign your whole site just to give non-desktop users a better layout. You can modify the CSS of your existing site to scale down the layout for devices with different screen sizes. In this half of the book, I'll walk you through taking traditional desktop CSS and adding in break points to give the site responsiveness on smaller screens. But before we start writing code, even though we're not doing a redesign, we need to spend some time thinking about the library website so we can make sure we're giving our patrons the best experience possible.

WHAT IS THE LIBRARY WEBSITE?

What is the library website? This seems like a strange question to ask, six chapters into a book on designing library websites. But libraries often have many different online tools that make up the library website: the home page and other pages in a content management system, the catalog, research databases, and discovery systems or federated search engines, to name a few. But many other tools, like link resolvers, interlibrary loan and course reserve software, audio and e-book services, as well as finding aids and research guides all fall under the umbrella of the library website.

This makes the job of maintaining a consistent visual design difficult, because each of these systems has its own default template, and some systems limit the amount of customization that you can perform. While the lessons for converting your site to a responsive design will apply to most of the online tools your library provides, exactly how you might modify these different interfaces could change depending on the system. In the last chapter of this book, I'll walk you through some advanced projects redesigning hosted vendor systems, including those that don't offer you many options for customization.

For now, though, we need to look at all of the services your library provides online through different interfaces. Do you have an online catalog? That's one online system. Interlibrary loan software like Illiad? That's another. How about providing audiobook or e-book downloads through Overdrive? Do you have a link resolver to connect patrons to articles in research databases? A federated search tool? Any special tool you've built in-house (like our Library Systems Status page at www.gvsu.edu/library/status). Make a list of all of these systems.

The most important system is the one that houses your home page. When people visit your library online, where do they go? Your CMS? Your catalog? Your LibGuides? This is the system you want to focus on first, since it is the first place your patrons come when they use the library website. In addition, starting with your home page will let you set the tone for redesigning your other online tools.

Some systems may be easier to change than others. For instance, if your site is hosted in a CMS or as static HTML pages and you control the template, then you won't have any trouble updating the styles of the site to make things responsive. But if you use a vendor product as your home page, then you'll have to work around the limitations of the software to make your design work. Likewise you may have to work with another department in your school or library to make changes to the website. This may limit the kinds of changes you can make, so be sure to talk to the vendor or someone knowledgeable about your site's infrastructure to make sure the changes you'd like to make are possible.

REVIEW YOUR ANALYTICS

Once you know where you are going to start, it's important to take a look at how people currently use your website. There are two aspects to this: how and why. Seeing how they use your site, which pages they visit, how long they stay, and which kinds of searches they do helps. But this information needs to be supplemented with talking with your users and understanding *why* they use your site and the kinds of problems they encounter in its use. Looking at your usage statistics is a great way to know which kinds of questions to ask your patrons, and it will also lead you to some surprising insights about the kinds of things your site gets used for.

There are many analytics services, but the most common is Google Analytics.[2] It's free, and it gives you a lot of detail about patrons who use your site as well as what they do, where they are, and which devices they use. If you aren't currently using any analytics program, you should look into setting up Google Analytics and letting it run for a few months. After a bit of time, you'll start to see patterns in the way your patrons move through your site, and you'll discover how your site really gets used.

One of the first things you should check in your analytics program is the bounce rate. This tells you how many people only looked at one page on your site, without ever continuing on to another page. This can tell you a lot, if your patrons need to move across several pages to complete common online tasks (like renewing a book or signing up for an event). If your bounce rate is high, you might be losing a lot of folks who can't figure out how to move on to complete their tasks. However, if your site is like Influx's "One Pager," a high bounce rate should be expected.[3] The site contains all of the library information and links on a single page! Likewise if your search tool takes you to a hosted vendor catalog or discovery service, you'll likely have an abnormally high bounce rate. If patrons come to your home page and use the search bar, the results will be displayed on a separate site, and your analytics program will count those visits as bounces, even though from the patron's perspective, he or she never left the library website.

If you do find that patrons are not venturing beyond the initial page they encounter on your site, never fear. Analytics will only get you so far. You can see that a problem exists, but you can't tell from these numbers necessarily *why* so many people are leaving after just one page. There are ways to find out what is causing the trouble, and in the next section we'll cover some of those tips.

Google Analytics also gives us an easy way to check in on how many "mobile" visits our site is getting. By checking in with this number regularly, you can have a good sense of how many patrons are trying to access your content on smaller screens, and it might prove useful for making a case for pursuing a solution like responsive design. In addition, it is fun to watch the mobile numbers climb once you do make your site responsive. Once folks realize that your site is easy to use on a phone or tablet, they'll start visiting more on those devices rather than waiting to get to a desktop computer. At GVSU, mobile traffic tripled in the first month after we went responsive. It was a good confirmation of what we already knew: that our patrons wanted to use our tools on whatever device they had handy at the time.

Also take a look at how people move through your site. You can see where they come from, how they move from page to page on your site, and where they go when they leave. This can be very instructive in understanding just how folks use your site. There are often many steps needed to complete common library research tasks, and they may take patrons through several different vendor systems to make the trip. For instance, at GVSU, many faculty, graduate students, and students who have declared a major will use subject-specific databases to start their research rather than the all-in-one bucket of our discovery service. This way they can start with a narrowed pool that is more targeted to the subject they are researching. But this path is hard to trace.

Once they leave the library database list on our CMS, they visit the database vendor's website. They perform their search and find many relevant articles, some of which are likely available in full text right through their database of choice. But this is not always the case. Often an article might appear as an abstract in a research database, but the full text is not available to the patron without checking other databases. From within the native database vendor interface, patrons can do a search "Find it @ GVSU," which brings them to a third system, our link resolver. This tool looks through all of our licensed databases and determines how many other places the article is available and whether any of them carry the full text.

If the patron is lucky, we'll have the full text in another database, and he or she can click the big "Read the Full-Text" button and be sent off to a fourth system, another database vendor site where the article awaits. Sometimes, however, we just don't have the full text available. They might then be directed to the library catalog to grab a copy in print or be whisked off to our interlibrary-loan software to place an order for a copy. This simple task of finding an article to read sends our unwitting patron through four different systems in various combinations, and it happens hundreds of times every day. By watching the analytics, you can begin to build a clear picture of how folks are moving from one tool to another, accomplishing (or failing to accomplish) tasks.

KNOW YOUR USERS: DON'T MAKE ASSUMPTIONS

It's easy to take the rich statistics that analytics services provide us and start making changes based entirely on the numbers. But we don't have the whole picture yet. Without understanding why our users are making the decisions reflected in the analytics data, we can't know the best way to make any changes to improve their chances of succeeding. We first need to find out what makes them tick.

Many of us spend a lot of time interacting with our patrons: at the circulation and reference desks, in instruction sessions or tutorials. We hear selected feedback from our patrons about how our online tools work for them or problems that they face. We work in the library; we know the ins and outs of our online tools and the best way for others to do research. It's easy to get stuck in the idea that we know what our patrons are thinking when they use our sites because of the knowledge we bring to our jobs.

But we don't. These anecdotal memories of ours aren't enough for us to really know what drives our patrons. We need to talk to them, to watch them use our websites, and just sit back and listen. User experience designer Whitney Hess says, "User experience isn't about expert intuition, it's about expert listening."[4] While we don't need to do everything our patrons suggest, it's important to let go of our ideas about how the website should work while we listen to them tell us about their experiences. After all, the library website is for patrons, not for library staff.

Interviews and Usability Tests

There are many structured tasks that you can do to get to know what is behind the patterns in your analytics data. But we've already covered how those of us who work in libraries are likely understaffed. We don't have time for dedicated usability testing rooms and other labor-intensive ways to get to know our users. Fortunately, doing user research doesn't have to be difficult. It just takes a few hours, not a few weeks.

Interviews are the easiest way to get feedback from your patrons. Ideally, you will schedule these ahead of time with a diverse group and meet with them one-on-one. Interviews aren't like focus groups, where you have a bunch of patrons come all at once for a group interview. Focus groups are great at getting at what people *like*, but they are not so great at telling you what people *do*. For that, we need to get people away from the influence of other, potentially more domineering personalities and ask them some simple questions about how they use the library.

You'll want to get a group of representative patrons to make sure that you are getting a sense of how many different types of people use your library site. If you are a public library, you'll want to figure out which demographic groups represent the bulk of your patrons. That may mean kids, teens, adults, and seniors, or it might be broken down by folks who check out books, those who get audiobooks and e-books, and members who take advantage only of events.

The types of questions you ask your patrons will vary depending on the tools your library provides and what you learned in your analytics gathering. You'll certainly want to ask them some questions about their lifestyle and how the library fits in to that. This can help you understand the type of patron you are dealing with. Be prepared to have your assumptions shattered when doing interviews!

Remember not to ask leading questions and also to avoid simple yes or no questions. The goal here is to learn more about how your site fits into your patrons' activities, how well it helps them achieve their goals and complete the tasks they need to do, and the problems they encounter when using it.

Interviews can be time consuming, especially if you want to reach a large portion of your patron population. I know librarians who have successfully created short five-minute interviews that they can ask patrons to participate in at the end of a reference interview or circulation desk transaction (if the library isn't too busy). The important thing is to spend a little time talking to the people who use (or should use) your website to find out how you can make it better for them.

If you have specific problems you know that you need to solve, a usability test might be a good place to start. Usability tests are a little bit like interviews, and you ask patrons to try doing a few common things on the library website. Then you just watch them. (Usually you watch them fail to do the thing that you thought would be easy.) Usability tests are excellent for finding out exactly where the roadblocks are that your patrons are facing as they try to use your site.

I've written a lot about how we do regular, monthly usability testing at Grand Valley,[5] but most of what I've learned about the subject came from Steve Krug's book *Rocket Surgery Made Easy*.[6] All you need to do a few usability tests is a computer that connects to the Internet and some patrons who are willing to try to complete a few tasks. It helps to give the patrons an incentive, like a T-shirt or free pizza. I've also seen a lot libraries successfully recruit testers by offering to forgive late fines.

At GVSU, we usually test three students a month on about four tasks. I start with a little interview, asking them some questions about themselves and how they use the web, both for fun and for school. This gives me a sense of how knowledgeable they are about the web, but it also helps them relax a little and feel more comfortable.

I then give them some simple tasks to do. The important thing here is to ask them to do actual things your patrons do, not things your administrators want people to do. I can't tell you how many libraries use a task like "find the borrowing policies" in their tests. No one looks up policies for the sake of policies! At the very least, the tasks need to be framed in a way that patrons can understand. Instead of asking them to find the policies, ask them to find out how long they can check out fiction books for. That's why they might actually encounter the policies in the first place.

It also helps to couch your tasks in little scenarios. The patron you are testing might not know why he or she would need to know how long a book can be checked out for, so you want to tell a little story to make it feel more real for the patron: You are going on vacation next week, on Monday, and will be gone for ten days, but you just got a notice that a newly released book, *Vampires in Love*, is being held for you. Find out if the book will be due before you return from your vacation.

The goal is to convince the patrons that they are doing a task that is as close to what they might do in their own lives. This will give patrons the context they need to poke around and try to complete the task. While they're clicking around trying to complete the task, just ask them to "think out loud." This little monologue will really give you insights into how they perceive your site and will probably surprise you.

You'll find that most of the folks you test will really enjoy this part of the usability test. I'm usually surprised by how disappointed our students are when I run out of tasks for them.

At GVSU we also have an observation room where library faculty and staff can observe the test in progress. We show the student's screen on a projector and play the conversation I am having with the student through speakers. Having these extra sets of eyes and ears guarantees that you'll find more problems than you will if you watch patrons by yourself. You can also record the sessions and play them back later if you're not able to do a real-time observation. Bringing in your coworkers has the added political benefit of showing everyone the problems with the website and getting everyone involved in identifying the solutions.

Once you have a handle on how your patrons use your site and why they do what they do, it's time to start using that knowledge to improve your site.

NOTES

1. That's how I changed the GVSU website in six months. You can see the progression in the video "Iterate, don't redesign," at http://vimeo.com/52561335.
2. Google Analytics, http://analytics.google.com.
3. Influx Library User Experience's OnePager is a free, one-page template for library websites, available at http://weareinflux.com/onepager.
4. Whitney Hess, "Don Draper Is the Antithesis of User Experience," February 27, 2012, http://whitneyhess.com/blog/2012/02/27/don-draper-is-the-antithesis-of-user-experience/.
5. Matthew Reidsma, "How We Do Usability Testing," November 15, 2011, http://matthewreidsma.com/articles/13.
6. Steve Krug, *Rocket Surgery Made Easy* (Berkeley, CA: New Riders, 2010).

Chapter Seven

Making Your Existing Layout Responsive

Once you have a good idea of what patrons are using on your site and what drives them, you can start thinking about converting your existing site to be responsive. However, at this point, if anything you uncovered during the initial research phase shows that crucial parts of your site either are going unused or are confusing patrons and causing them to fail to complete their tasks, you'll need to address those issues before you move on. No design polishing or cross-device compatibility makes up for an unusable website.

Your website will have some issues—all sites do. If the problems are relatively minor and most of your patrons are still able to do what they need to do, you can move ahead. The goal here is to make the transition to a responsive website without redesigning your whole site and, if possible, not making any drastic changes except in the case where the existing site prevents patrons from doing what they need to do.

So far, this book has been largely theory, a description of how responsive design works and some minor discussions of practically putting these techniques into practice. But for a better understanding of how to make the conversion from a fixed-width to a fluid, responsive site, we're going to get our hands dirty. I've created a run-of-the-mill library home page, with elements similar to what you might have on your home page. The site is online at http://matthewreidsma.com/rwd, and I'll be using it as a template for converting a fixed-width library site into a responsive one. But don't worry—you don't need to be online to make use of this section. I'll include all of the relevant code snippets and techniques, as well as plenty of screenshots to make sure you can see how the changes I suggest affect the final site.

ARE YOU USING A GRID?

Since responsive web design starts with a flexible, grid-based layout, we need to first look over your site's layout to see whether it is already grid-based. If you remember from chapter 2, grids are proportional structures that help give structure to a page. While your library site's design might have a visual structure, there is a good chance it's not strictly a grid, since it isn't proportionally divided. Rather, our library sites usually fit content in wherever there is room. To convert our existing site to a responsive design, we're going to have to fine-tune our site's layout and make sure it is laid out on a grid.

Take a look at the Awesometown Public Library home page (figure 7.1). There is a lot of content on the page, and the layout is structured in columns throughout the header, navigation, main content, and footer. We might at first think that this home page is grid based, but if we look carefully, we can see that there are some problems involving proportions in the columns.

When laying out a grid on a print project, designers have the constraint of the page size for determining the type and size of the grid they will use. But on the web, we don't have this kind of constraint. We do, however, have the content for our site, which in some cases has fixed or minimum useful sizes. So rather than using the outer boundary of our page to define our constraint, we'll use the content that will make up the page to help us define our grid.

A quick review of the page shows two roughly equal larger columns in the header, six equal columns in the navigation bar, three columns of slightly different sizes in the main content area below the slideshow, and two columns separated by a third empty column in the footer. To accommodate all of these various layouts, then, we need to build a grid with columns divisible by 2, 3, and 6. We could go with six columns, which would map perfectly onto our navigation bar. Or we could use a twelve-column grid. The goal is to have all of the content elements on the page fit within one or more of the columns so that all of the elements are sized proportionally to one another. I'll stick with a simple six-column grid.

If we add the grid to the home page, we can see that our current layout is not quite proportional (figure 7.2).

FIGURE 7.1

Our existing Awesometown Public Library home page.

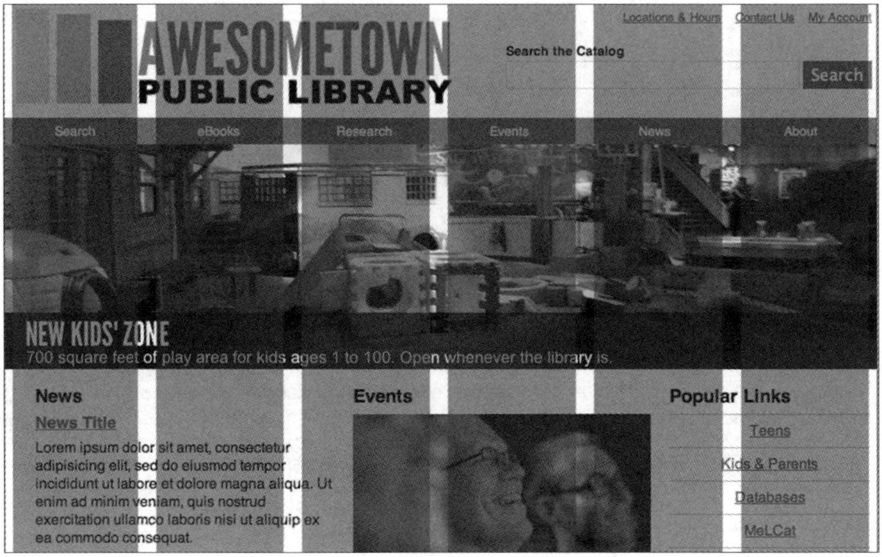

FIGURE 7.2
Oops, we're not quite grid-based yet.

Let's first look at the header. The library's logo sits over on the right, stretching just beyond three columns width. The top navigation and search bar on the left feel like the right size but are pushed to the right by the logo stretching across the center. If we look at the CSS for the page, we'll see that the logo is intended to be slightly larger than half of the page:

```
body {
    margin: 0 auto;
    width: 960px;
}
#logo {
    float: left;
    width: 500px;
}
#top-navigation,
#search-catalog {
    float: right;
    text-align: right;
    width: 420px;
}
```

In this case, the `#logo` is no longer proportional to the page, since its 500-pixel width does not fit snugly into the columns. If we want to fit the header into our new six-column grid, then we'll need to fit the `logo` into the columns proportionally. We could extend the logo to fill four columns, but that would force us to drastically shrink the catalog search box, which I think is more important than a gigantic logo.

We can also shrink the width of the logo to fit within three columns, or exactly 50 percent of the width of the page. We can resize the image to maintain the same height in our favorite image editor, or we can just have the browser resize it by changing the size of its container. Since we're hoping to make this conversion quickly, I'll let the browser handle resizing the image, even though this will change the height of the header.

FIGURE 7.3
Our newly resized logo fits into three grid columns.

Since each column is 150 pixels wide with 5 pixels of padding on both the left and right, we'll want our logo to line up with the right edge of the third column, not including the padding. This means we are building a single column that spans half the width of our page, with 5 pixels of padding on either side (figure 7.3). Our new CSS looks like this:

```
body {
     margin: 0 auto;
     width: 960px;
}
#logo {
     float: left;
     padding-left: 5px;
     width: 470px; /* 480 - 5 - 5 = 470 */
}
#top-navigation,
#search-catalog {
     float: right;
     padding-right: 5px;
     text-align: right;
     width: 470px;
}
```

Note that I have declared the padding only on the edges of the page, and not the padding between the two floated columns. Because we are floating one column to the left and another to the right, the padding in the center will take care of itself. By specifying the padding on the edges of the page, the content chunks will be in the right place, and by leaving the center flexible, browsers that round pixel values differently will have some wiggle room when putting the layout together.

However, since the form was sized to fit inside a smaller container, we need to adjust some widths to accommodate for the larger right column in the header. Here was our old form CSS:

```
#search-catalog form {
    margin: 24px 5px 0 15px;
    width: 400px;
}
#search-catalog form input[type="text"] {
    border: 1px solid #ddd;
    font-size: 18px;
    padding: 4px;
    width: 320px;
}
#search-catalog form input[type="submit"] {
    background-color: #093;
    border: none;
    color: #fff;
    font-size: 18px;
    padding: 5px 0;
    width: 76px;
}
```

We'll want to calculate the new widths of these items, but since we know we are ultimately going to make these values proportional rather than fixed, let's just go ahead and do that now. The `#search-form` container was originally 420 pixels wide. Let's use our formula `Target ÷ Context = Result` to get proportional values from these old styles. Our new CSS looks like this:

```
#search-catalog form {
    float: right; /* Make sure the form aligns to the right */
    margin: 1.5em 0 0;
    width: 95.238095238095%;
    /* 400 ÷ 420 = 95.238095238095% */
```

```
}
#search-catalog form input[type="text"] {
     ...
     font-size: 1.125em; /* 18 ÷ 16 = 1.125 */
     padding: .25em 1.25%; /* 4 ÷ 320 = 1.25% */
     width: 80%; /* 320 ÷ 400 = 80% */
}
#search-catalog form input[type="submit"] {
     ...
     font-size: 1.125em;
     padding: 0.3125em 0; /* 5 ÷ 16 = .3125 */
     width: 19%; /* 76 ÷ 400 = 19% */
}
```

Now our header is complete, with everything aligning properly on a grid.

Moving down the page, we can see that the navigation elements line up perfectly on our grid, as does the slideshow, which fills the width of the page. However, the main content area below the slideshow shows some proportion problems (figure 7.4), which we can see are intentional once we look through the CSS:

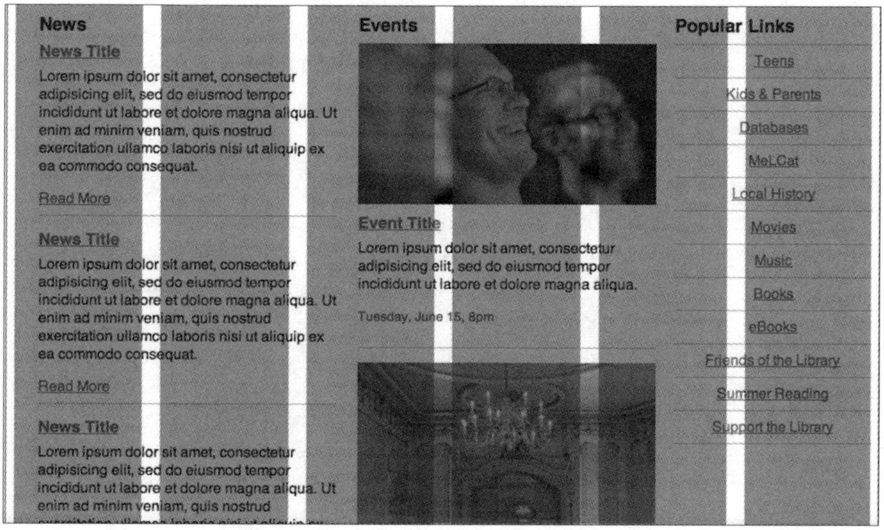

FIGURE 7.4
It's not clear what these columns line up with.

```
#news,
#events,
#popular-links {
     float: right;
}
#news,
#events {
     padding: 8px 12px;
     width: 350px;
     }
#popular-links {
     padding: 8px;
     width: 235px;
}
```


The news and events columns are nearly a third larger than the list of popular links. There isn't a particularly obvious reason for this difference, other than perhaps links being less important than the news and events information. But if this is the case, why are the links on the page at all? We can presume that all of these pages are available through the site's main navigation, so there must be a compelling reason to have secondary navigation on the page. If there is, it should be given equal weight to the content that surrounds it.

If we were using a twelve-column grid, we might consider having the links be two columns wide, and then spitting the remaining ten columns between the news and events. But with a six-column grid, I think making each of the three content areas the same width is the best option. In that case, each content area will span two columns, with 5 pixels of padding on either side. Our CSS can be simplified to this:

```
#news,
#events,
#popular-links {
     float: right;
     padding: 5px;
     width: 310px.
}
```

At this point, the page is looking more organized than before, simply by tweaking each of our content areas to fit inside a grid. But the address on the right hand bottom of the page is not quite properly in the grid (figure 7.5). It looks like the text starts right in the middle of one of the columns.

FIGURE 7.5
The address doesn't really line up with anything.

If we were using a twelve-column grid, that might work fine, but in our six-column grid, we should line up the address container with our columns. In our old CSS, there was plenty of room to the left of the `#address` container:

```
#social-media {
     float: left;
     padding: 12px 8px;
     width: 500px;
}
#address {
     float: right;
     padding: 12px 8px;
     width: 250px;
}
```

Here we need to convert the styles to make the social media section the width of three grid columns, while the address column will cover just two:

```
#social-media {
float: left;
width: 470px;
}
#address {
float: right;
width: 310px;
}
```

Looking at our site now, we can see that the layout is very similar to our original design, but the pieces all fit together a little better, thanks to the typographic grid (figure 7.6).

Converting this single page to a grid was fairly easy, but doing an entire site may be more of a challenge. One useful trick is to use techniques developed by Nicole Sullivan for writing "Object Oriented CSS" (OOCSS).[1] The premise behind OOCSS

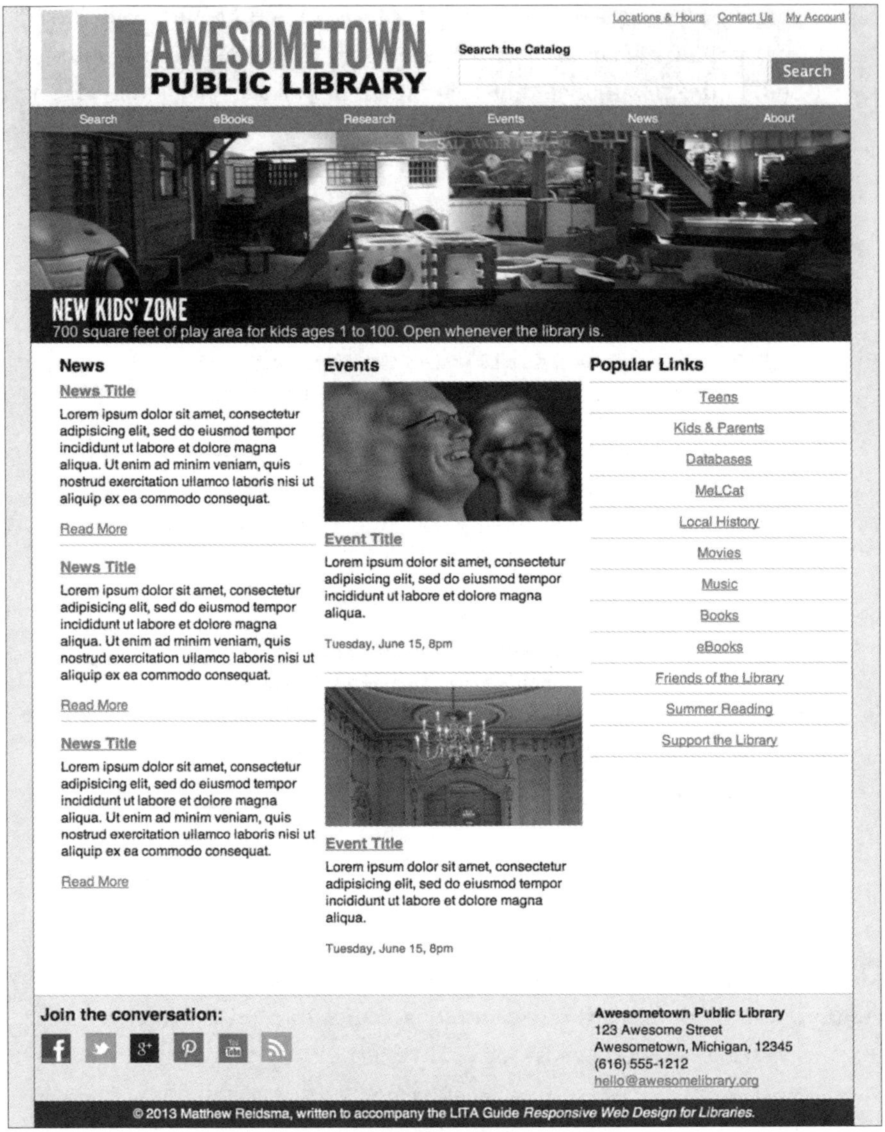

FIGURE 7.6

Everything seems just a little more organized on the grid.

is that by using descriptive classes that each have one or maybe two styles, you can make creating new content that fits to your grid much easier.

As an example, earlier we used the style `float:right` for several unique IDs. By using OOCSS, we can add one CSS class to our styles, like `.float-right`, and then assign this class to each of those elements that need to be floated right. The benefit of reusing styles this way will become apparent once we start thinking through how content containers with different IDs but similar styles need to be changed with media queries. Here's an example of how we might change the markup and CSS from our last example to use OOCSS:

```
<!-- Markup changes -->
<div id="social-media" class="float-left column3 column">
    <!-- Content here -->
</div>
<div id="address" class="float-right column3 column">
    <!-- Content here -->
</div>

/* Styles for OOCSS conversion */
.column {
    padding: 12px 5px;
}
.column3 {
    /* column3 = you can fit 3 columns across. */
    width: 310px;
}
.float-left {
    float: left;
}
.float-right {
    float: right;
}
```


If you have to deal with a lot of different online tools, building a system that contains easily reusable styles will be invaluable. At Grand Valley, I built a User Interface Pattern library based on OOCSS to enable us to easily create new content that matches the grid and typographic styles of all of our other systems. You can see our pattern library online at http://gvsu.edu/library/ui, and even download the stylesheet we use to see how an OOCSS framework is made and modify it for your own library. I'll talk more about how useful this pattern library is in chapter 9.

To simplify the process of teaching you how to convert your site to a responsive design, however, I'll continue using IDs in my styles to make sure that the connection between the CSS I am walking you through and the content you see on the screen is explicit.

CONVERTING EXISTING STYLES INTO A RESPONSIVE STYLESHEET

Now that we have made sure our existing library home page layout is based on a grid, we are ready to get rid of all of those fixed-width values keeping our site from being beautifully fluid. We'll use the formula `Target ÷ Context = Result` to convert our fixed-width layout into a fluid one, just like we did a moment ago with our search form. Let's start with the header, examining the HTML source so we can see how the elements of the header are nested within the page:


```
<!-- Header and logo -->
<div id="header" role="banner">
     <div id="logo" role="heading">
          <a href="index.html">
               <img src="img/logo.png" alt="Awesometown
Public Library" />
          </a>
     </div>
     <div id="top-navigation" role="navigation">
          <ul>
               <li><a href="#">My Account</a></li>
               <li><a href="#">Contact Us</a></li>
               <li><a href="#">Locations &amp;
Hours</a></li>
          </ul>
     </div>
</div>
<div id="search-catalog">
     <form role="form">
          <label for="search">Search the Catalog</label><br />
          <input type="text" name="search" id="search" />
          <input type="submit" value="Search" />
     </form>
</div>
```

Here we can see that the `body` element is the container (or, in the words of our formula, the context), by which we'll find the relative widths of our content elements.

Let's take a look again also at the CSS we wrote when we converted the layout to a grid:

```
body {
     margin: 0 auto;
     width: 960px;
}
#logo {
     float: left;
     padding-left: 5px;
     width: 470px;
}
#top-navigation,
#search-catalog {
     float: right;
     padding-right: 5px;
     width: 470px;
}
```

Converting the widths of our content containers to relative widths should be simple here. Our context is 960 pixels, the width of the `body` element. And in every case, the target width of our content containers is 470 pixels. Our formula for finding relative widths for these elements will be `Target ÷ Context = Result`, or:

$$470 \div 960 = 48.958333333333\%$$

Now we need to calculate the relative value of the padding. Remember that in the case of padding, the context is not the width of the containing element but the width of the element itself.[2] In that case, our formula to find the relative value of the 5 pixels of padding will be:

$$5 \div 470 = 1.063829787234\%$$

So now we have all of the relative values we need to make our header layout fluid. We just need to swap out our old fixed-width declarations for our new relative values:

```
#logo {
     float: left;
     padding-left: 1.063829787234%;
     /* 5 ÷ 470 = 1.063829787234% */
     width: 48.958333333333%;
     /* 470 ÷ 960 = 48.958333333333% */
}
#top-navigation,
#search-catalog {
     float: right;
     padding-right: 1.063829787234%;
     text-align: right;
     width: 48.958333333333%;
}
```


Now that our header has been converted to fluid, relative widths, we can move on to the rest of the site. Our navigation was already a nice fit for our new grid, but the widths of the elements are decidedly fixed. All it takes is a quick look at the CSS to get the values we need for our relative width conversion:

```
#main-navigation ul li {
     background-color: #093;
     display: inline-block;
     float:left;
     font-size: 14px;
     padding: 8px 0;
     text-align: center;
     width: 160px;
}
```

This conversion is pretty straightforward, since we don't have to worry about padding or margins. Instead, we just need to change the width of the navigation elements into relative values. Our context here is the `#main-navigation <div>`, which is set to 100 percent of its parent, the `<body>` element. So our formula is as follows:

$$160 \div 960 = 16.666666666667\%$$

Our new CSS width for our navigation elements would then be:

```
#main-navigation ul li {
    …
    font-size: 0.875em;
    padding: .5em 0;
    width: 16.666666666667%;
}
```

So far, if we reload the page, our site looks exactly as it did after we converted it to a fixed-width grid. That's because we're just changing out one value for an equivalent value.

Our slideshow already takes up 100 percent of the width of the `body` element, and so by simply adding a max-width to all `<img>` elements, we can make those fluid as well:

```
img {
    max-width: 100%;
}
```


Moving down to our three columns of content and the `#address` area, we can use one formula to convert them all, since they are all the same width. Our formula for making these all relative is as follows:

310 ÷ 960 = 32.291666666667%

Within the "Events" column we have images, but thanks to the rule we added for our slideshow earlier, those images will be constrained to the width of the column.

Our social media container is the same width as the logo, 470 pixels, so we can just borrow the relative width, 48.958333333333%, from there. However, the context of the padding has changed, so we can't just use the same padding as on the address element. Our new horizontal padding (8 pixels) is calculated with this formula:

8 ÷ 470 = 1.702127659574%

It's also a good idea to convert our font sizes and vertical margins and paddings to ems, so that everything on our page is proportionally sized. Since we used a reset stylesheet on our site and declared the font size of the `<body>` element, we know that 1 em is equal to 16 pixels. We can use our simple formula to convert our fixed measurements to ems by using 16 pixels as the context, as in this example for the `padding` and `font size` for the `#main-navigation`:

Padding: 8 ÷ 16 = .5 ems

Font size: 14 ÷ 16 = 0.875 ems

However, horizontal padding should be calculated in percentages, since we want to make sure that padding remains relative to the width of the viewport. For the margins in the social media and address sections, we'd use the following formula, since the context is the element itself and not the container:

12 ÷ 310 = 1.612903225806%

After converting all the horizontal margins and padding, our final CSS with relative widths for all of our content containers looks like this:


```
body {
     margin: 0 auto;
     width: 960px;
}
img {
     max-width: 100%;
}
#logo {
     float: left;
     padding-left: 1.063829787234%;
     /* 5 ÷ 470 = 1.063829787234% */
     width: 48.958333333333%;
     /* 470 ÷ 960 = 48.958333333333% */
}
#top-navigation,
#search-catalog {
     float: right;
     padding-right: 1.063829787234%;
     text-align: right;
     width: 48.958333333333%;
}
#top-navigation ul {
     font-size: .8em;
     list-style-type: none;
     margin-top: .5em;
}
#top-navigation ul li {
     display: inline;
     float: right;
     margin-left: 3.191489361702%;
```

```
}
#main-navigation ul li {
    background-color: #093;
    display: inline-block;
    float:left;
    font-size: 0.875em;
    padding: .5em 0;
    text-align: center;
    width: 16.666666666667%;
}
#news,
#events,
#popular-links {
    float: right;
    padding: 0.3125em 1.612903225806%;
    width: 32.291666666667%;
}
#address {
    float: right;
    padding: .75em 1.612903225806%;
    width: 32.291666666667%;
}
#social-media {
    float: left;
    padding: .75em 1.702127659574%;
    width: 48.958333333333%;
}
#social-media ul li {
    display: inline;
    margin-right: 2.162162162162%;
}
```


And our site looks exactly the same as it did before (figure 7.7). Unfortunately, even when we make the viewport smaller, it looks the same as it did before. It doesn't flex or move when the viewport resizes. Didn't we just do all of this work to make our site fluid and flexible?

In our new responsive stylesheet, the `<body>` element is still set to a fixed width. So even though our other elements are sized proportionally to the `<body>` element, because the `<body>` element is a fixed width, no other elements will change as the viewport resizes. The solution is to make the `<body>` fluid, sized relative to the viewport.

FIGURE 7.7

At the same viewport size, our proportionally-sized site looks identical to the fixed-width version.

Currently, the `<body>` is set at a fixed width of 960 pixels, and the margin styles make sure that this fixed container is centered on the viewport if it is larger than 960 pixels. We want to retain this behavior for larger screens, so we want to think about how to write our styles so that the `body` doesn't grow larger than 960

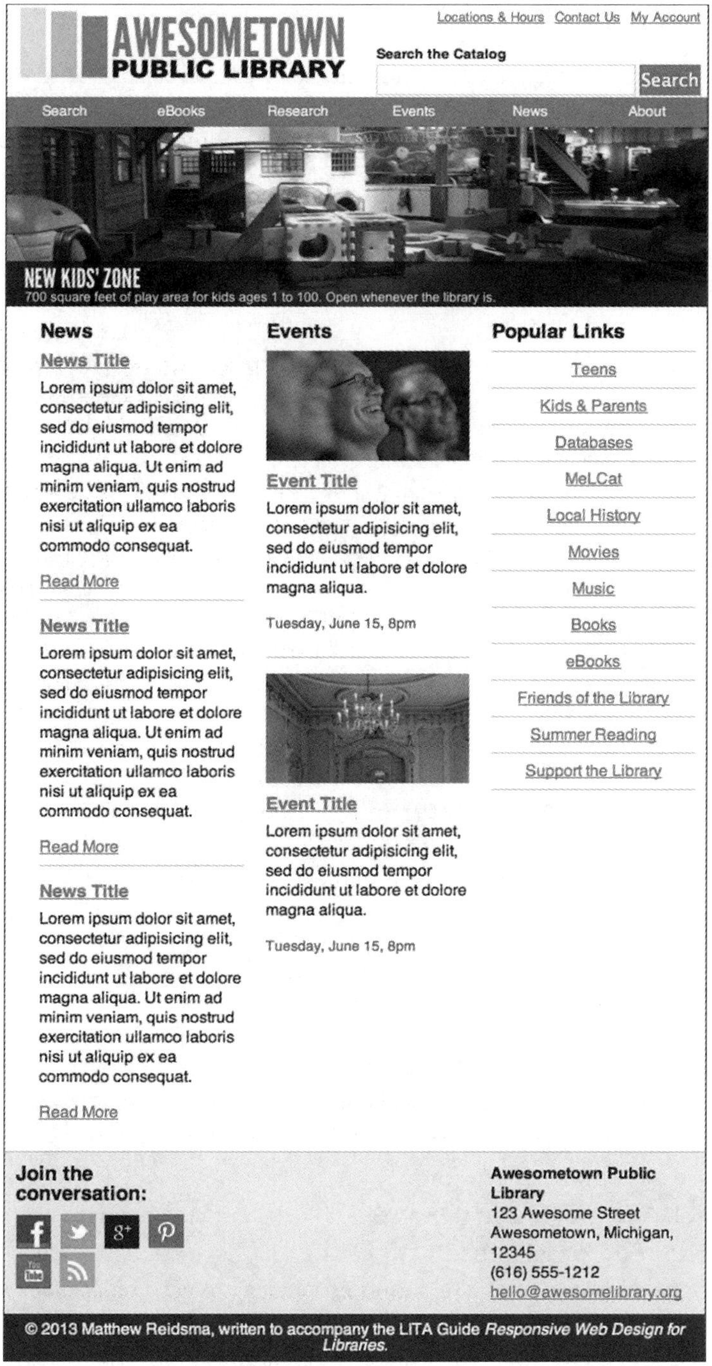

FIGURE 7.8
On smaller viewports our site is fluid.

pixels and stays centered on the screen. Once the viewport drops below 960 pixels, however, we'll want the <body> to stretch to fill the entire viewport. We can do this will two simple changes to our stylesheet:

```
body {
     margin: 0 auto;
     max-width: 60em; /* 960 ÷ 16 = 60em */
     width: 100%;
}
```

Instead of sizing the <body> at a fixed width, we'll change the value to 100 percent of the viewport, but we'll set a maximum width of the relative equivalent of 960 pixels. So now, when the viewport reaches a size over 960 pixels, the size will behave as it did when it was fixed width, but below that point will be fluid and flexible (figure 7.8).

PLANNING FOR LAYOUT AT SMALLER SCREEN SIZES

It hasn't taken us long to convert our library home page to a fluid grid, ready to handle different viewport sizes without hiding or shrinking content. But unfortunately our site isn't really optimized for smaller screens. In fact, below a viewport of about 775 pixels, our site starts to look crowded (see figure 7.8). We can't rely solely on the content being proportionally sized; we'll need to add some media queries to rearrange content a bit on smaller screens.

But before we start adding in media queries, we need to think a little about how our content will behave on smaller screens. In the first half of the book, I argued that it's a good practice to start with a small screen, linear layout and then start moving content into columns once you have more real estate in the viewport to play with. But in our case here, we already have a layout for large screens. We need a way to adapt to smaller viewports.

We've already noticed that things start to feel compressed at viewports around 775 pixels. In the header, the search bar doesn't have enough breathing room under it. Although our content columns are starting to get smaller, they don't yet feel *too* small. At the bottom of the page, our address is starting to take on more rows than we'd like. So in our first break point, we need to just make some minor adjustments to the header and footer.

The logo and the search form are lining up in a way that is distracting, with the bottom of the logo landing at about the vertical center of the form's input field. Since the height of the header is set by the height of `#logo`, it gets smaller as the image proportionally resizes itself to smaller viewports. This makes positioning it to line up with the search form a challenge.

But while we can't easily make the two items line up while remaining fluid, we can make the alignment less obvious for the current viewport size. In our original stylesheet, we added 1.5 ems of margin to the top of the `form`. By simply reducing that amount to .75 ems, we'll minimize the effect of the misalignment, by having the bottom of the input field above the bottom of the logo. We'll likely have to make other adjustments as the viewport continues to shrink, but this is a good start.

Next, we want to make some adjustments to the width of `#search-form` so that it doesn't wrap onto a second line or the search button doesn't feel too scrunched. We have a few options here. We could remove the search form from the right header column and have it span the whole width of the site above the navigation. We could also get fancy and use JavaScript to hide the search bar until an icon, like a magnifying glass, was clicked, but in this case let's keep it simple.

Since 800 pixels is still a lot of room for a single input field to cover, the best option is to adjust the spacing around the form and the size of the text on the search button.

First, we'll want to give some more space below the search form on these smaller viewports. But since the elements in the header are all floated without a wrapper, setting a fixed bottom margin for the whole area can be tricky. Instead, we'll add some padding to the `#main-navigation` section below the form, which will give us enough extra room to make the form feel less cramped:

```
#main-navigation {
    padding-top: 1em;
}
```

The text of the search button is another matter. We could adjust the `font size`, but then we would also have to adjust the relative padding, since the em value would change. Instead, let's switch from a text search box to an icon of a magnifying glass. This is a pattern that has become increasingly common on smaller viewports. We'll want to make sure that our search label remains for assistive devices and toggles to the image without switching the markup of the page from a submit to an image button. We can do it all with CSS:

```
#search-catalog form input[type="submit"] {
    /* Add a background image of the search icon */
    background-image: url(img/search.png);
    background-repeat: no-repeat;
    background-position: center center;

    /* Hide text visually while keeping it accessible */
    text-indent: -9999px;
}
```

We now have a search button that has more leeway horizontally as it flexes with our fluid layout (figure 7.9).

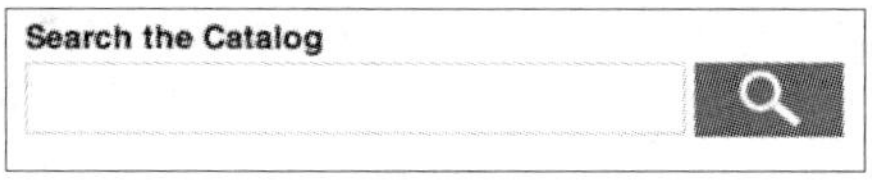

FIGURE 7.9
At small screens, we'll use an accessible icon for our search button.

Our header now looks better on smaller viewports, but we're developing some layout issues in the footer. Our address just doesn't have enough horizontal room, so parts of the address are wrapping. The address is still legible, and it doesn't affect the ability of our patrons to find the address, but visually we expect addresses to be formatted a certain way. All we need to do is give the container a little more room to breathe.

The best solution is to increase the width of the address container to fill three grid columns, the same as the social media container. Of course, we also need to update our relative padding, since the container size has changed. Our new styles for the address container look like this:

```
#address {
    padding: .75em 1.702127659574%;
    width: 48.958333333333%;
}
```

Since all of these issues came up at viewports around 775 pixels wide, we need to wrap the new styles in a media query set to work on viewports smaller than that. But remember, we want to make our media queries in ems, to better support the flexible site we've worked so hard to build (figure 7.10). So here is our first media query, which we include below the rest of our CSS in our layout stylesheet:

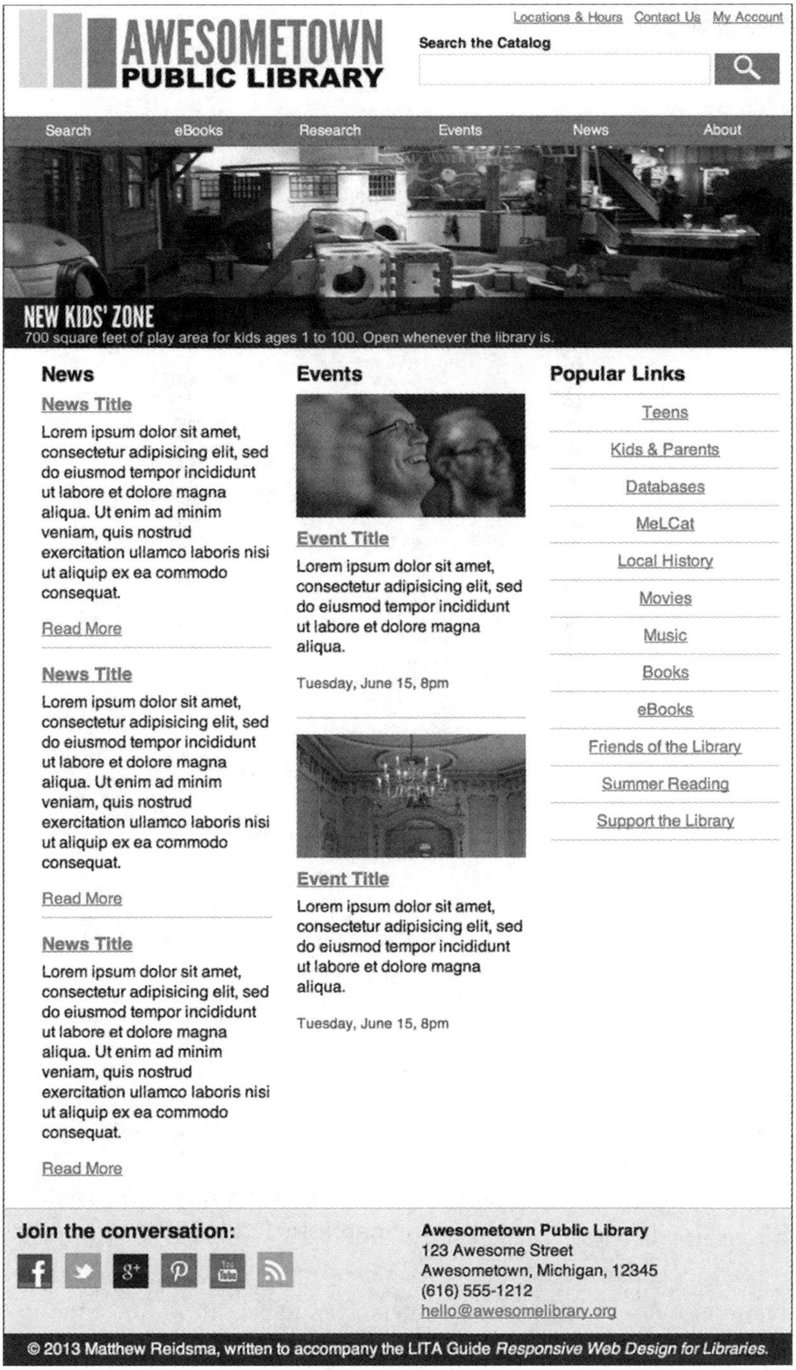

FIGURE 7.10

With our first media query, we've made small adjustments that keep our fluid site usable.

```
@media screen and (max-width: 48.4375em) {
    /* 775 ÷ 16 = 48.4375 */

    #main-navigation {
        padding-top: 1em;
    }
    #search-form form {
        margin-top: .75em;
    }
    #search-catalog form input[type="submit"] {
        background-image: url(img/search.png);
        background-repeat: no-repeat;
        background-position: center center;
        text-indent: -9999px;
        }
    #address {
        padding: .75em 1.702127659574%;
        width: 48.958333333333%;
    }
}   /* End 48.4375em media query */
```


As we continue to scale down the viewport, our next problem shows up around 700 pixels (figure 7.11).

First, the logo is starting to get smaller, and it's feeling really cramped in that upper left corner. We need to give it a little bit of room to breathe. Moving down the page, we really need to do something about our three content columns. At 700 pixels, each is just over 225 pixels, and the text and images are all feeling the pinch. Finally, the lower footer is starting to wrap, and that looks a little odd with the centered text.

First we'll add about 12 pixels worth of margin above the logo, just to keep it from feeling like it was disappearing into the top of the page. Then we'll left justify the lower footer and give it a small amount of padding around the text to make it more legible when it spans the entire width of the viewport.

The major change comes from the content areas. Since the popular links come first in the source order, we'll have them span the entire width of the viewport, splitting from a single column of links into three equal columns. We'll want to add a class to two of our last list items, since we want the whole bottom row to have borders on the bottom. In our original styles, we already added a bottom border to the last item. So the end of our list in the markup will look like this:

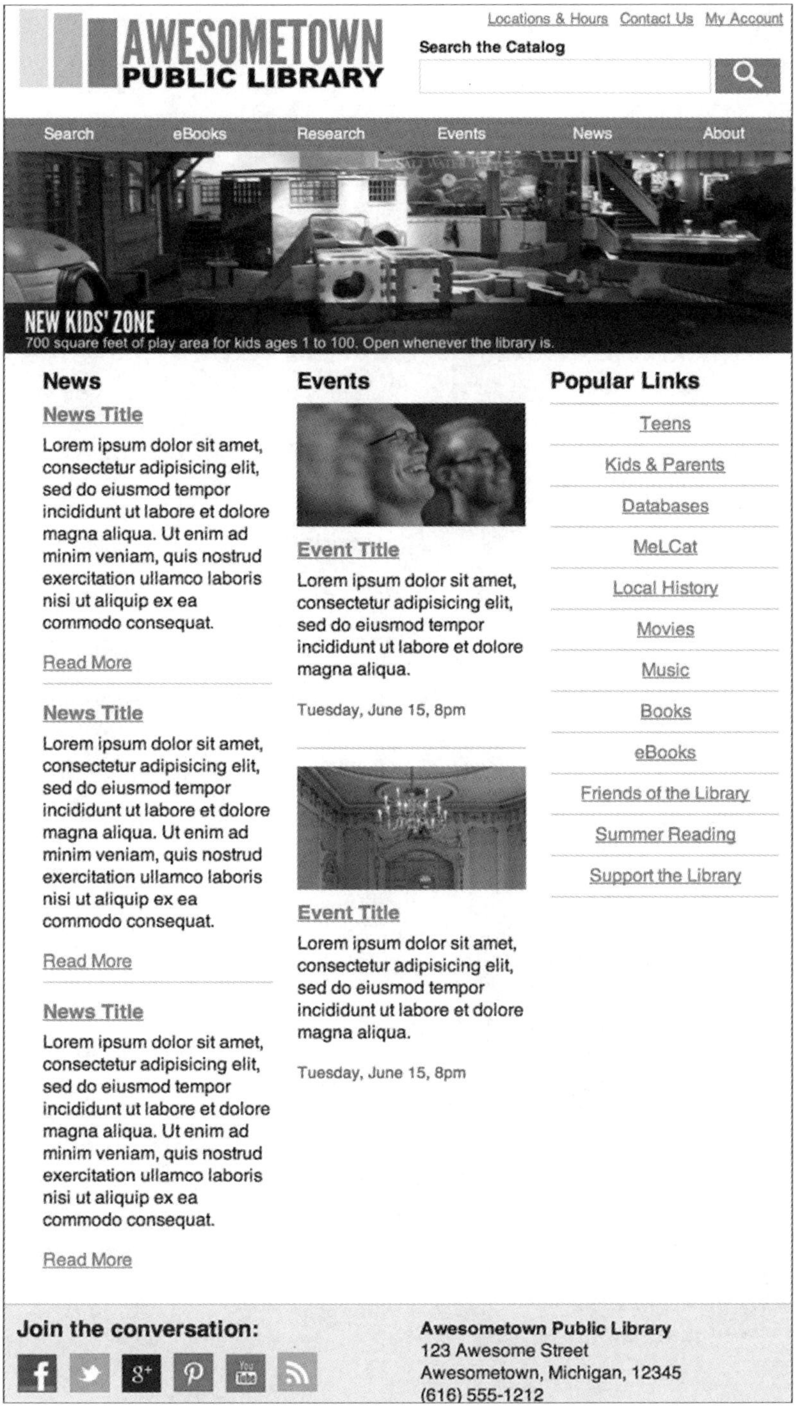

FIGURE 7.11
Now things are getting tight at 700 pixels.

```
...
    <li>
        <a href="#">eBooks</a>
    </li>
    <li class="bottom-row">
        <a href="#">Friends of the Library</a>
    </li>
    <li class="bottom-row">
        <a href="#">Summer Reading</a>
    </li>
    <li>
        <a href="#">Support the Library</a>
    </li>
</ul>
```


Then we'll give the news and events sections a little more room, having them span three grid columns each. That will make the whole page feel more legible (figure 7.12). Our new media query, set to trigger at 700 pixels, looks like this:

```
@media screen and (max-width: 43.75em) { /* 700 ÷ 16 = 43.75 */
    #logo {
        margin-top: .75em;
    }
    #popular-links {
        float: none;
        width: 100%;
    }
    #popular-links ul li {
        float: left;
        margin-right: 0.520833333333%;
        width: 32.291666666667%;
    }
    #popular-links ul li.bottom-row {
        /* Add this class to markup */
        border-bottom: 1px solid #bbb;
    }
    #popular-links ul li a {
        text-decoration: none;
    }
    #news,
    #events {
        margin-top: 1.5em;
        width: 48.958333333333%;
```

```
    }
    #footer-bottom p {
        line-height: 1.4em;
        padding: .25em 2%;
        text-align: left;
    }
}
```

As the viewport continues to drop, the social media icons in the footer wrap at around 615 pixels. At that point, it's time to make the social media section and the `#address` stack on top of each other instead of floating side by side (figure 7.13). This can be done with a quick media query:

```
@media screen and (max-width: 38.4375em) {
    #social-media,
    #address {
        float: none;
        width: 100%;
    }
}
```


Once the viewport is down to 590 pixels, the header is again appearing cramped. It's time now to pull the search form of the right side and have it fill the width of its container. Once the search form drops down, however, it's clear that the top navigation links need some space above them. They feel like they are stuck to the top of the page, while the logo next to them has room to breathe. By adding a small margin and aligning the top of the text with the top of the logo's text, we'll make the header feel more organized and usable on this size viewport:

```
@media screen and (max-width: 36.875em) {
    #top-navigation {
        margin-top: 1em;
    }
    #search-catalog {
        float: none;
        clear: both;
        width: 100%;
    }
}
```

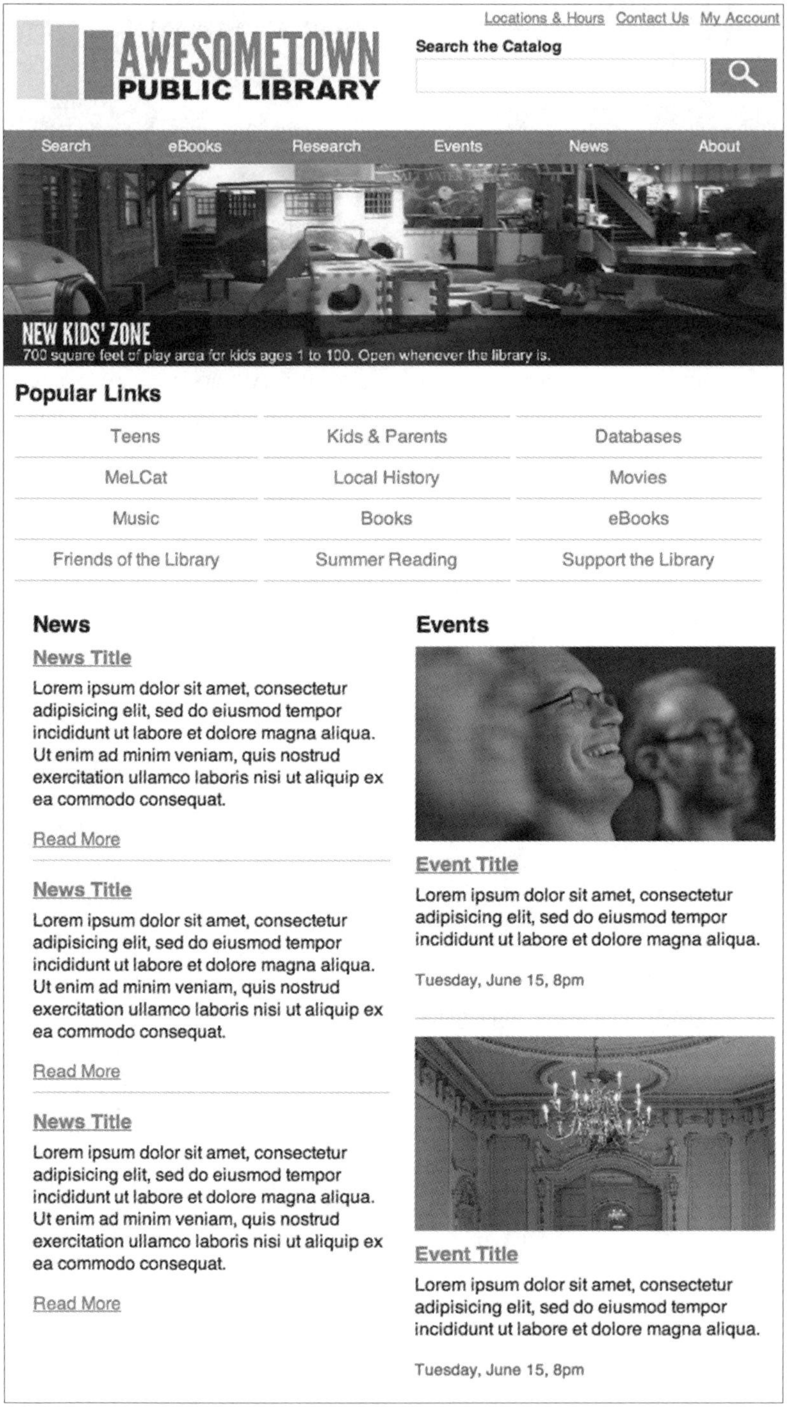

FIGURE 7.12
A little rearranging and things are looking better.

FIGURE 7.13
Logo/text in viewport

FIGURE 7.14
Links in vertical list

Just a smidge smaller and the top navigation starts to wrap. Now we need to think through how to handle these commonly used links. While one common design pattern for these types of links is to create a drop-down menu with an icon, an easier solution is to stop floating them and let them sit in a vertical list with a 1-em margin at the bottom of each item (figure 7.14). The Apple Human Interface Guidelines suggest a 44-pixel square as a touch target, and these links are well under that with about 32 pixels of vertical space, so we could increase the font size and add a bit more margin to the spacing between the links. Because this will stretch the header vertically a bit, we can take back some of the horizontal space we allocated for the links and give it back to the `#logo` (figure 7.15). The new media query looks like this:

```
@media screen and (max-width: 36.25em) {
     #top-navigation {
          width: 32.291666666667%; /* 2 grid columns */
     }
     #top-navigation ul li {
          display: block;
          float: none;
          font-size: 1.125em; /* 18px */
```

```
        margin-bottom: 1.33333333333333em;
        /* 24 ÷ 18 = 1.33333333333333em */
        margin-right: 5px;
        text-align: right;
    }
    #logo {
        /* 4 grid columns */
        width: 66.145833333333%;
        /* 635 ÷ 960 = 66.145833333333% */
    }
}
```

Once the viewport drops to 550 pixels, the content columns of the news and events are getting a bit crowded. It's time to stop floating these columns and stack them on top of one another. That's easy enough with a simple media query:


```
@media screen and (max-width: 34.375em) {
    #news,
    #events {
        clear: both;
        float: none;
        width: 100%;
    }
}
```

Our event images are now quite a bit larger than they've ever been before (figure 7.15). We'll have to make sure that the images are at least 550 pixels wide to accommodate this size viewport. In the next chapter, we can talk about strategies for optimizing these images so that they don't put an excessive burden on larger viewports, where the image is displayed at a fraction of this size.

Our site is looking quite organized now, even though we have lost significant horizontal space. As the viewport gets down to about 515 pixels, our three rows of popular links breaks, and it's time to switch to two rows. We can do this simply by changing the width of the list elements, removing the bottom border on the list items that were in the bottom row in three columns, and adding a border to the list items in the bottom row with two columns. This means adding another class in our markup to the second-to-last list item, so that the end of the `popular links` list looks like this:

FIGURE 7.15
The extra viewport gets smaller, but the content gets bigger.

```
...
    <li>
        <a href="#">eBooks</a>
    </li>
    <li class="bottom-row-3">
        <a href="#">Friends of the Library</a>
    </li>
    <li class="bottom-row-3 bottom-row-2">
        <a href="#">Summer Reading</a>
    </li>
    <li>
        <a href="#">Support the Library</a>
    </li>
</ul>
```


This media query is quite simple, and gives `#popular-links` more room horizontally on the smaller viewport (figure 7.16):

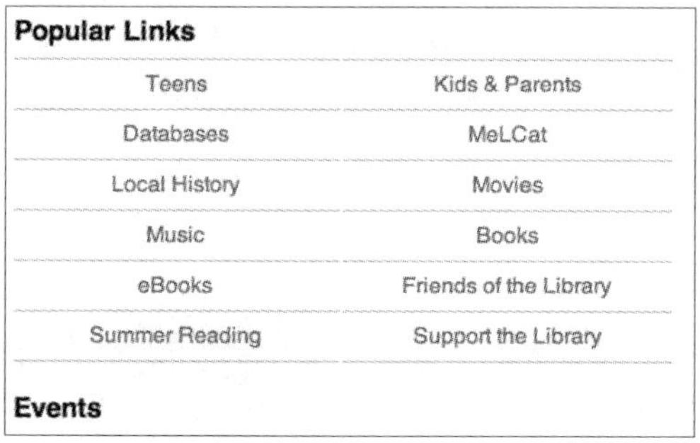

FIGURE 7.16
The popular links now split the viewport in half.

```
@media screen and (max-width: 32.1875em) {
    #popular-links ul li {
        width: 48.958333333333%;
    }
    #popular-links ul li.bottom-row-3 {
        border-bottom: none;
    }
    #popular-links ul li.bottom-row-2 {
        border-bottom: 1px solid #bbb;
    }
}
```

Our viewport is getting quite small, but we still have some room to go. Once the viewport drops down to around 500 pixels, all of the navigation at the top of the screen becomes largely unusable. The main navigation bar is smooshing links together, and the top navigation links are running into the logo and beginning to wrap. It's time to make the navigation more usable on small screens.

Let's tackle the main navigation bar first. These links are already nice, touchable blocks of green with white text. Instead of floating them next to each other as we've done on larger viewports, let's stack them atop one another like block elements. We simply need to stop floating them and set their width appropriately. And since they will now be atop one another, we'll add a border between each to help differentiate them:

```
#main-navigation ul li {
    border-bottom: 1px solid #fff;
    display: block;
    float: none;
    width: 100%;
}
```


But this change to the CSS has some unexpected consequences (figure 7.17). The list elements seem to just run right over the top of the slideshow and down into the popular links area. Looking back to the largest viewport we designed for, we set an explicit height on the list element's parent, the `<ul>`, to help fill any gaps in the width of the horizontal list. So once the main navigation moves to block-level elements, we need to remove that height declaration and let the browser set the height of the lists:

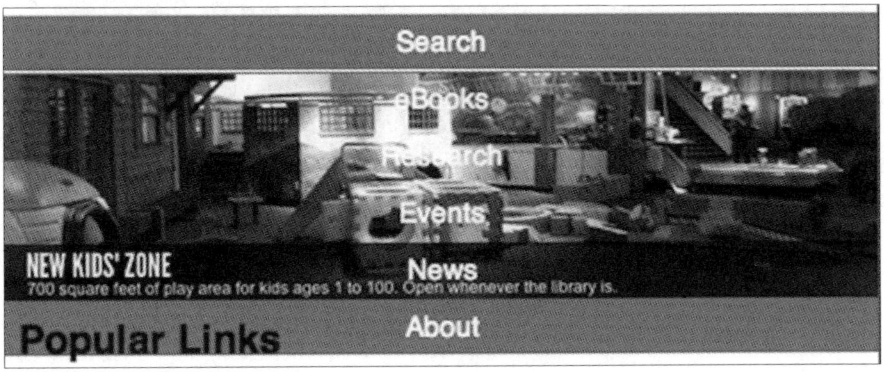

FIGURE 7.17
Well, that's not what we expected.

```
#main-navigation ul {
    height: auto;
}
```

To fix the crowded header, we need to stop floating the logo and the top navigation links next to one another. We'll move the top navigation below the logo and go back to floating each link in a horizontal line. Because we declared a top margin earlier on our logo, we'll need to remove that. Now our site elements are all usable at this smaller viewport size (figure 7.18):

```
#logo,
#top-navigation {
    float: none;
    margin-top: 0;
    width: 100%;
}
#top-navigation ul li {
    display: inline;
    float: right;
}
```


Our site actually scales down quite well to the lowest viewport settings now. If we were to go much below 320 pixels, we'd probably need to break the popular links into a single column, which we could do by changing the width of each list element to 100 percent and negating the floats. But all in all, we've done a pretty decent job of converting an existing website from fixed-width to responsive, in not all that much time.

Of course, this is not the most refined responsive design. The site on small viewports is full of chunky lists of links that sit above the site's main content. The slideshow proportions look a little crummy on small viewports, and the text embedded in the image is hardly readable. But remember, this site wasn't designed with small viewports in mind. If we had the time (and political clout), we'd start thinking about changing the site to a mobile-first design, building our media queries up from a clean, linear layout as we enhanced the site as the viewport increased. But because you probably can't do that right now, we'd made due with what we have.

We've really changed the way our patrons can access our site, whether they are on a mobile device or a desktop computer with a small browser window (figure 7.19). And while we could certainly rest on our laurels at making the site's layout

FIGURE 7.18
The navigation is much more usable as a vertical list at this viewport size.

FIGURE 7.19
Our site is much more accessible now (right) than it was before (left).

adapt to changing conditions, our site still hasn't been optimized to perform well, regardless of device. In the next chapter, we'll tackle that.

NOTES

1. Nicole Sullivan, "Object-Oriented CSS," http://oocss.org.
2. Remember also that we're using a CSS `box-sizing: border-box` rule to make padding part of the declared width of the element, rather than in addition to the width. If you're not using `box-sizing: border-box` because of browser support issues, you'll need to adjust the declared widths to account for the extra padding.

Chapter Eight

Improving Your Site's Performance

Our library home page is now accessible to all of our patrons, regardless of the device they use. But there are areas where we could still improve performance.

To work through many of these changes, I've moved each media query we created in the last chapter into its own CSS file. This gives us ten CSS files, counting our base "layout" CSS we used when creating the large-viewport version of the site and the reset stylesheet we used to make sure all browsers started from the same place in rendering our styles.

TESTING EXISTING PERFORMANCE

There are several ways to test your site's performance, but the easiest is to use the built-in Web Inspector tools included with most browsers.[1] In Google Chrome, the Inspector is available from the contextual menu, which appears when you right- or option-click on an item. By bringing up the contextual menu on any element in your website, you can access the Inspector, which will open the guts of the page and show you all of the HTML, CSS, and JavaScript (as well as any problems) that make that element appear and behave as it does.

In Chrome, we can open the Inspector on our library home page and switch to the Network tab. Once we reload the page, this tab will show us the size and loading time of each of our page's assets (figure 8.1). If we want to understand

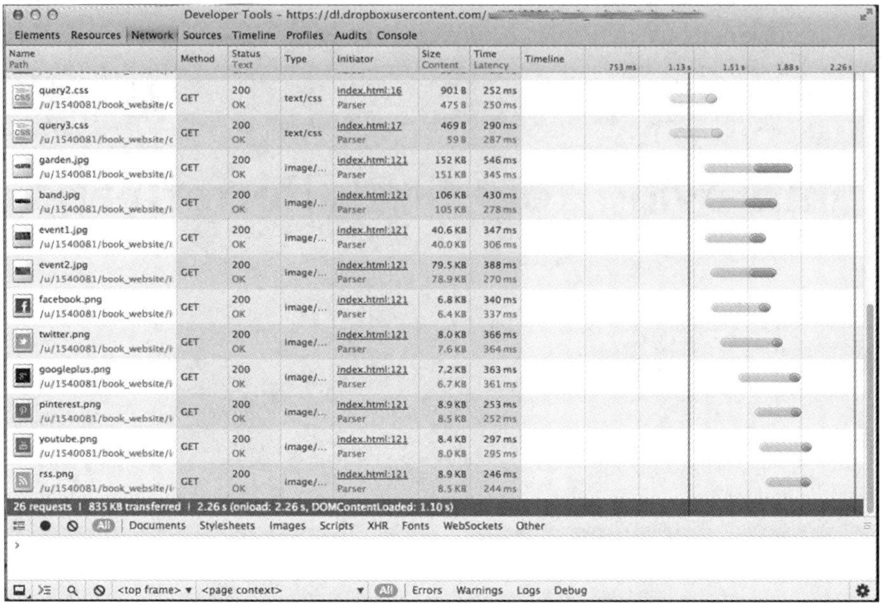

FIGURE 8.1
The Inspector's Network tab gives us a detailed overview of our site's performance.

how well our site performs, this is where we start. We will see not only our file sizes and load times but also where bottlenecks occur, or which assets are being loaded from a sluggish server.

When we look at our page, we see that we have twenty-six requests, for a total of 841 kb. Since the average size of a webpage as I am writing this is 1485 kb, we're still falling under that.[2] But remember, our CSS and JavaScript are only serving a single page, and we're limiting our slideshow (where the bulk of the page weight lives) to three slides. I haven't seen many slideshows on library websites with so few slides, so we're a little unusual in that regard.

But let's not pat ourselves on the back just yet. We learned to adapt break points to our content rather than to arbitrary device widths, because it improved the experience for all patrons. We should also aim to make our sites as efficient as possible, regardless of what the "average" webpage might or might not do.

So we have a lot of work ahead, reducing both the bytes we send and the number of requests we make. We'll tackle the easy stuff first and then look at ways to make our sites perform better even when JavaScript fails.

COMBINING AND MINIMIZING STYLES AND SCRIPTS

At the beginning of this chapter, I made separate CSS files for each of our media queries. Each of those files takes time to load as the browser waits for the server to respond. Since the media queries for this version are in the `<link>` elements, we need to change the structure of our markup a bit to call just one CSS file instead of ten. Our former markup was as follows:

```
<!—Stylesheets -->
<link href="css/reset.css" rel="stylesheet" type="text/css" />
<link href="css/layout.css" rel="stylesheet" type="text/css"»
  media="screen"  />
<link href="css/query1.css" rel="stylesheet" type="text/css" »
  media="screen and (max-width: 48.4375em)" />
<link href="css/query2.css"  rel="stylesheet" type="text/css" »
  media="screen and (max-width:43.75emem)" />
<link href="css/query3.css" rel="stylesheet" type="text/css" »
  media="screen and (max-width:38.4375em)" />
<link href="css/query4.css"  rel="stylesheet" type="text/css" »
  media="screen and (max-width:36.875em)" />
<link href="css/query5.css" rel="stylesheet" type="text/css" »
  media="screen and (max-width:36.25em)" />
<link href="css/query6.css"  rel="stylesheet" type="text/css" »
  media="screen and (max-width:34.375em)" />
<link href="css/query7.css" rel="stylesheet" type="text/css" »
  media="screen and (max-width:32.1875em)"/>
<link href="css/query8.css" rel="stylesheet" type="text/css" »
  media="screen and (max-width:31.25em)"/>
```

We're going to move everything to a single stylesheet, including the reset styles. To do that, we change our markup to the following:

```
<!-- Stylesheets -->
<link href="css/styles.css" media="screen" rel="stylesheet" »
  type="text/css" />
```

This will load the styles.css stylesheet instead of all of the existing files, but that means we need all of the existing styles to be in this new styles.css file. We'll start by moving the old stylesheets into the file in the order they were loaded before.

At the top of our stylesheet we'll put our reset styles, followed by the contents of layout.css. After that, we'll include each query stylesheet, wrapped this time in an inline media query. In the end we'll have one CSS file that is larger than any of our previous files but keeps us from doing nine additional server requests.

The new CSS structure has us down to seventeen server requests but is transferring nearly the same amount of data, 837 kb. The page looks the same, but we were able to keep the patron's browser from asking for more files than it needed.

Of course, we can also minimize our CSS file, stripping white space and comments. When I run our new styles.css through a CSS minimizer like http://csscompressor.com, I can compress the CSS file by 53 percent, dropping from nearly 11 kb to just under 5 kb. Our page is now down to 831 kb served across seventeen requests.

Next we can look at our JavaScript files. We're loading the jQuery library to run our slideshow, but we're loading the full, uncompressed jQuery library at 268 kb. One fast solution is to switch to the minimized version of jQuery, which drops the file size to 91 kb.[3] This has the immediate effect of dropping the number of bytes we are serving to our patrons to 654 kb, which is 22 percent smaller than the webpage we started with. And we've only just begun.

We can optimize this JavaScript library even further. First, we could use a slideshow script that doesn't require jQuery, which would remove the need for the library at all. But let's assume that we need jQuery for more than just running a slideshow on our home page. If we use a minimized version of jQuery from a content delivery network (CDN) like Google's Developer Libraries, we can take advantage not only of their very fast servers but also of browser caching.[4] By switching our jQuery call to load from Google, we drop the size of the transferred file from 91 kb to 33 kb, bringing our page size down to 596 kb. But more important, since many other sites use the Google CDN, there is a good chance that your patron may have already downloaded this jQuery file from Google. That means his or her browser will use the cached version stored on the computer instead of loading a new one.

We're also loading two other files: a plugin by Mat Marquis for a responsive slideshow and then our own scripts file that calls the slideshow. Both are in separate files and neither is compressed. By putting both of these in the same file, `scripts.cat.js`, we can drop down to sixteen server requests. By minimizing this script, we can cut down to 588 kb.

The `<head>` of our home page now looks like this, with our CSS, meta elements, and scripts all loading before the `<body>` of the file is parsed:

```
<head>
    <meta name="viewport" content="width=device-width, »
      initial-scale=1" />
    <title>Awesometown Public Library</title>
    <!-- Stylesheets -->
    <link href="css/styles.min.css" media="screen" »
      rel="stylesheet" />
    <!-- Scripts -->
    <script src="//ajax.googleapis.com/ajax/libs/ »
      jquery/1.10.2/jquery.min.js"></script>
    <script src="js/scripts.cat.min.js"></script>
</head>
```

However, there is another performance issue in this structure that we can fix. Since we are loading our JavaScript files in the `<head>`, browsers will not start any new downloads while the JavaScript files are being downloaded. This can cause a bottleneck as our other page assets build up, and if JavaScript fails to load at any point, it could prevent our patrons from seeing the home page. To clear this problem, then, we'll move our scripts to the bottom of our document, right above the closing `<body>` tag. While this doesn't change the number of requests or the number of bytes sent, it does make the page start rendering faster.

OPTIMIZING IMAGES

The largest portion of our home page is now images, which account for twelve of the sixteen requests and 533 kb of the total bytes sent. More than half of the images won't change regularly during the course of the site's life span, since they are social media icons and the logo. The other five images will likely change, since they constitute the slideshow and the images advertising upcoming events.

The quickest way to achieve some savings on our images is to run them through an image compressor. On the Mac, I use ImageOptim,[5] but there is also a great web-based tool at www.smushit.com. Both are free, and handle all sorts of images with ease. By dragging and dropping the twelve images we have on our home page into ImageOptim, I can automatically save 81 kb, without any other optimization techniques (figure 8.2).

One option we have with the images that will live on the site permanently is to use an image sprite to do a single server request for one image that contains all

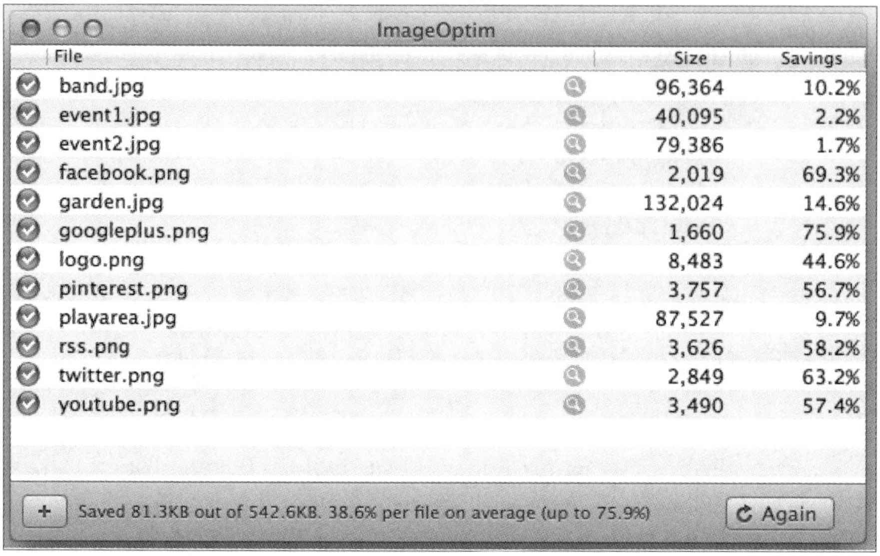

FIGURE 8.2
By optimizing images, we can reduce image size quickly.

of those icons and other images and use CSS to position the sprite to show only the image we want. Sprites cut down not just on server requests but also on bytes, since they are generally smaller files than all the individual images taken together.

But sprites require us to use CSS background images, rather than in-line `<img>` elements, and this has a semantic consequence. CSS background images are great when the image has no semantic meaning to the patron reading your site: background images and textures, decorative elements, and the like. But when the image itself is content and conveys meaning, then you should use an `<img>` element with an appropriate `alt` attribute. In this case, our logo and social media icons do convey meaning. The images themselves tell you the name of the library and the social media accounts we have. Here, we should stay with inline `<img>` elements.

One thing we can do is see how large our source images are and what the largest size they will be displayed in our fluid site. When we examine the social media icons, they are never shown larger than about 36 pixels square. But the source images are sized at 66 pixels square! If we resize these social media icons to match the size they will be displayed, we can find some more savings. Resizing these icons down a mere 30 pixels vertically and horizontally drops the size of the Facebook icon from 7 kb to only 2 kb! While not all of the original icons were 7 kb, it still drops the size of each one to a manageable 2 kb. By simply resizing a few images, we save more than 20 kb.

We can do the same with our event images. They are currently 800 pixels across, and on some medium-sized viewports, they stretch to fill the width of the site. If we look at our media queries, we can see that we start spreading the event images to the full viewport width at 34.375 ems, or 550 pixels. There is no reason for these images to be more than 550 pixels wide, so by resizing them, we can find some more savings. Our first event image, of a man laughing, drops from 40 kb to 36 kb, and the photograph of a chandelier drops from a whopping 79 kb to 58 kb.

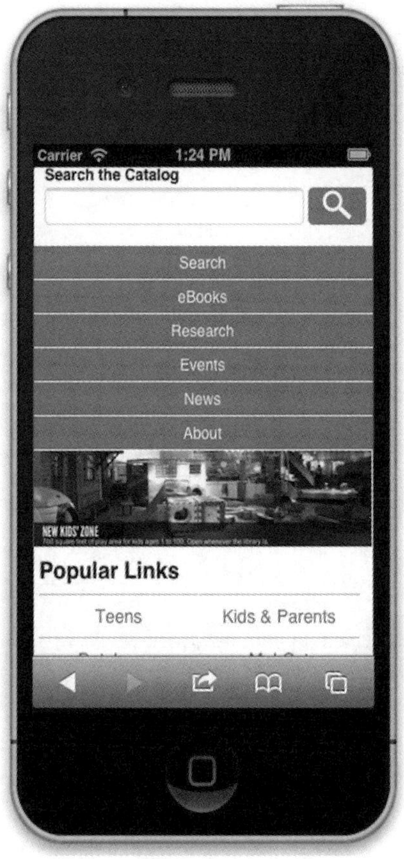

FIGURE 8.3
The text in our slideshow is laughably small on smaller viewports.

With these simple tricks, we've already dropped the size of our website from 841 kb to just over 540 kb. There are certainly more sophisticated tricks we could use to reduce the overall size of our site, but we've come a long way. Yet other than optimizing the images, we haven't even touched the slideshow, which accounts for most of the weight of our page.

We can't reduce the physical dimensions of the images, since they need to be 960 pixels wide to accommodate large viewports. However, each of our images has a translucent band across the bottom with text embedded in the image. While these titles are easily readable by patrons using visual browsers with large viewports, the text becomes a muddled mess on small viewports (figure 8.3). While we can use `alt` tags to provide the text inside the image to patrons with low vision and other assistive devices, it might be better for both accessibility and performance to use regular text positioned on top of the image with CSS. This will give us smaller image files, readable text on smaller viewports, and content that is readable by everyone, not just patrons with visual browsers.

Let's take a look at our slideshow syntax:

```
<ul class="slider" id="sliderName">
    <li class="slide">
        <img src="img/playarea.jpg" alt="Creative »
          Commons photograph by Ryan Somma »
          http://www.flickr.com/photos/14405058 N08/ »
          5970650764" />
    </li>
    <li class="slide">
        <img src="img/garden.jpg" alt="Creative Commons »
        photograph by Earthworm on Flickr at »
        http://www.flickr.com/photos/earthworm/130338986" />
    </li>
    <li class="slide">
        <img src="img/band.jpg" alt="Creative Commons »
          photograph from Infrogmation of New Orleans at »
          http://www.flickr.com/photos/29350288@N06/ »
          3139330979" />
    </li>
</ul>
```


The first step is to break the text out of the image and make it part of the markup:

```
<li class="slide">
    <img src="img/playarea.jpg" alt="Creative Commons »
      photograph by Ryan Somma http://www.flickr.com/ »
      photos/14405058@N08/5970650764" />
    <div class="slide-text">
          <h4>New Kids' Zone</h4>
          <p>700 square feet of play area for kids ages 1 to »
            100. Open whenever the library is.</p>
    </div><!-- End .slide-text -->
</li>
```

After removing the text from the image itself, we've managed to shave the image size down from 88 kb to 72 kb. But now the text falls below the slide, breaking our

FIGURE 8.4
Now the caption sits below the image.

layout (figure 8.4). We need to add CSS styles to position the text over the image, exactly where it was before:


```
.slide {
    position: relative;
}
.slide-text {
    background: rgb(0, 0, 0);
    /* Use transparency if supported */
    background: rgba(0, 0, 0, 0.7);
    bottom: 0;
    color: #fff;
    padding: 2%;
    position: absolute;
    width: 100%;
}
.slide-text h4 {
    font-size: 120%;
}
```

What we've done is similar to the trick we used for fluid media in chapter 2. We relatively position the parent element, in this case, the list element, and then absolutely position the text within that container. By positioning it at the bottom with percentage-based widths and paddings, we've ensured that it will scale nicely as the viewport size changes. Now our text is readable regardless of the viewport size, although the image is covered up by text on small viewports (figure 8.5).

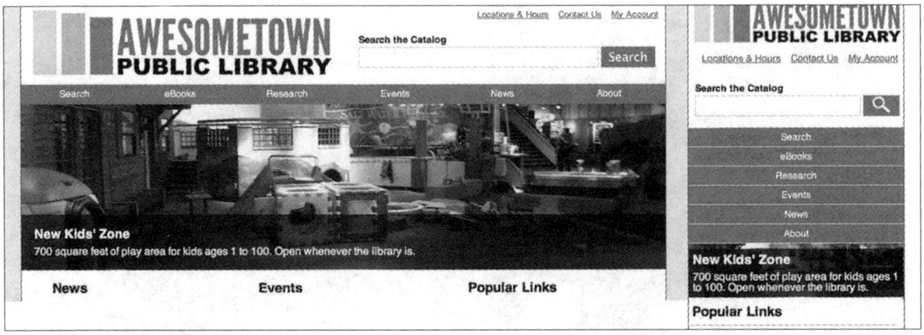

FIGURE 8.5
The text is now readable on any device, although the image is obscured on smaller viewports.

If we watch the slideshow as we scale down our viewport, we'll see that around 36.25 ems (580 pixels), the text starts obstructing too much of the image to make the image useful. We can simply create some new styles for this media query that will move the text below the image (figure 8.6).

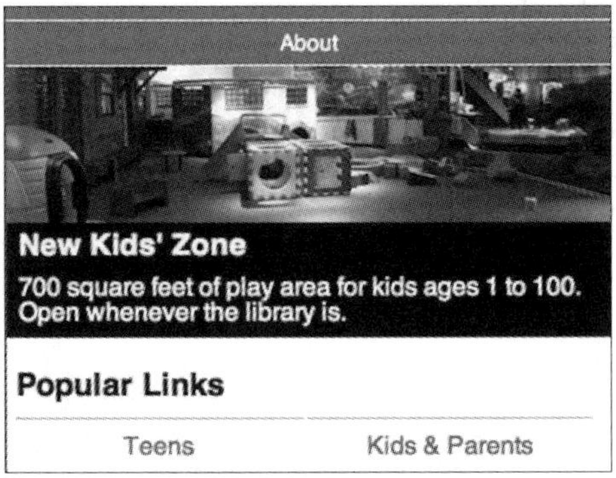

FIGURE 8.6
Now the text is below the image, and both are available to small viewports.

```
@media screen and (max-width: 36.25em) {
    .slide,
    .slide-text {
        position: static;
    }
```

```
    .slide-text {
        background: #000;
        margin-top: -.25em;
    }
}
```

Once we switch over all three of our slideshow images, we've dropped another 78 kb.

But there is still a performance upgrade we can achieve by making our slideshow images media aware. While we wait for the `<picture>` element, we can use a polyfill like Scott Jehl's Picturefill to help us load appropriate images depending on viewport size.[6] Even though we need to load more JavaScript, the savings we can achieve on smaller viewports is remarkable. For instance, on our first image, by loading a 400-pixel-wide image on small viewports instead of the 960-pixel-wide default, we save 55 kb. The smallest image size is a mere 17 kb, and all we need is to create several image sizes and change the markup in our slideshow.

First, we'll create and optimize four versions of each of our slideshow images: an original at 960 pixels wide, one at 800 pixels, one at 600 pixels, and one at 400 pixels wide. We'll then change from an in-line `<img>` element to Picturefill's `<span>`-based markup, with a fallback loading an `<img>` element for when JavaScript fails or is not available:

```
<li class="slide">
    <span data-picture data-alt="Creative Commons »
      photograph by Ryan Somma http://www.flickr.com/ »
      photos/14405058@N08/5970650764">
        <span data-src="img/playarea-small.jpg"></span>
        <span data-src="img/playarea-md.jpg" »
          data-media="(min-width: 401px)"></span>
        <span data-src="img/playarea-lg.jpg" »
          data-media="(min-width: 601px)"></span>
        <span data-src="img/playarea.jpg" »
          data-media="(min-width: 801px)"></span>
        <!-- Fallback content for non-JS browsers.
        Same img src as the initial, unqualified source
        element. -->
        <noscript>
            <img src="img/playarea-small.jpg" »
              alt="Creative Commons photograph by Ryan »
              Somma http://www.flickr.com/photos/ »
              14405058@N08/5970650764" />
```

```
        </noscript>
        <div class="slide-text">
            <h4>New Kids' Zone</h4>
            <p>700 square feet of play area for kids ages »
              1 to 100. Open whenever the library is.</p>
        </div>
    </span>
</li>
```

While this adds complexity to our markup, the performance benefits are worth it. Patrons with large viewports will not see any performance savings from this solution, but the real benefit is seen by devices with small viewports. On an iPhone in portrait, instead of loading all three full-size images for 240 kb, the three smaller images sent will be just 51 kb, a savings of almost 190 kb, or 79 percent! On small viewports, then, instead of sending 462 kb, we'll send just 272 kb. That's just over a quarter the size of the webpage we started with, and none of the performance optimizations we've done has been difficult or time consuming.

Our site is now fluid and responsive to all sorts of devices, and that flexibility is reflected in the way our site performs. But there are a few cases where we may still be inflicting unnecessary bandwidth that we can address.

Because our slideshow images are right in our markup, they'll load whether or not JavaScript is available. While it's true that most people have JavaScript available on their device, it's still liable to break or not execute properly on a device. When that happens, thanks to the <noscript> fallbacks of the Picturefill script, the patron will still see the slideshow images. But the slideshow itself will not work, and so the site content will be pushed

FIGURE 8.7
If JavaScript fails, we have a bunch of images stacked atop one another.

below all three of our images stacked atop one another (figure 8.7). In this case, one image would have sufficed. The extra images only make sense if JavaScript is both available and working properly. Fortunately, we can easily make a few changes that will keep an image in the markup for everyone, and then enhance the experience with a slideshow with multiple images for patrons with JavaScript.

First, we'll remove the last two images from the markup, so that by default only one image will load. Then, if JavaScript is working properly, we'll add the next two images with JavaScript before firing up Picturefill and the slideshow. Our new markup looks like this:

```
<ul class="slider" id="sliderName">
    <li class="slide">
        <span data-picture data-alt="Creative Commons »
          photograph by Ryan Somma http://www.flickr.com/ »
          photos/14405058@N08/5970650764">
            <span data-src="img/playarea-small.jpg"></span>
            <span data-src="img/playarea-md.jpg" »
              data-media="(min-width: 401px)"></span>
            <span data-src="img/playarea-lg.jpg" »
              data-media="(min-width: 601px)"></span>
            <span data-src="img/playarea.jpg" »
              data-media="(min-width: 801px)"></span>
            <noscript>
                <img src="img/playarea-small.jpg" »
                  alt="Creative Commons photograph by Ryan »
                  Somma http://www.flickr.com/photos/ »
                  14405058@N08/5970650764">
            </noscript>
            <div class="slide-text">
                <h4>New Kids' Zone</h4>
                    <p>700 square feet of play area »
                      for kids ages 1 to 100. Open »
                      whenever the library is.</p>
            </div>
        </span>
    </li>
</ul>
```

Now, after we load the jQuery library but before we load Picturefill and the slideshow code, we'll simply insert the HTML that creates the last two slides. Here's the simplified code for the second slide and the start of the third (line breaks added for clarity):

```
$("#sliderName").append('
    <li class="slide">
        <span data-picture data-alt="...">
            <span data-src="img/garden-small.jpg"></span>
            <span data-src="img/garden-md.jpg" »
              data-media="(min-width: 401px)"></span>
            <span data-src="img/garden-lg.jpg" »
              data-media="(min-width: 601px)"></span>
            <span data-src="img/garden.jpg" »
              data-media="(min-width: 801px)"></span>
            <noscript>
                <img src="img/garden-small.jpg" alt="...">
            </noscript>
            <div class="slide-text">
                <h4>Get Ready to Garden</h4>
                <p>Check out our huge selection of »
                  gardening books and videos, or sign up »
                  for our gardening club.</p>
            </div>
        </span>
    </li>
    <li class="slide">...
');
```


Now when our website loads, as soon as JavaScript begins to execute, it adds these items to the HTML, runs Picturefill to convert them to the proper images, and then turns the nice list of images into a slideshow. If JavaScript fails (or isn't available), the patron sees just a single image, and the site works as they would expect. Best of all, they don't have to download the extra images that aren't any use to them.

Now our site is optimized in terms of performance, and it looks great on nearly every device. Best of all, we didn't have to redesign the site to make these changes. We worked with our existing HTML and made minor changes that added up to big improvements for everyone.

NOTES

1. You might need to activate "Developer" mode in your browser to see the Inspector. There are also add-on inspectors, like Firebug, that you can install, but I use the Google Chrome Inspector in this chapter, since it's what I am most comfortable with.
2. HTTP Archive, "Trends," http://httparchive.org/trends.php.
3. This is available pre-minimized from jQuery, at http://jquery.com.
4. Google, "Google Hosted Libraries—Developer's Guide," https://developers.google.com/speed/libraries/devguide.
5. Kornel Lesiński, "ImageOptim," http://imageoptim.com.
6. Scott Jehl, "Picturefill," GitHub, https://github.com/scottjehl/picturefill.

Making Vendor Sites Responsive

While our library's home page is certainly responsive, the home page isn't necessarily the "library website." Behind the scenes, your library site probably consists of half a dozen or more vendor sites that work in tandem with your home page to make the library's online presence functional and useful for your patrons. When converting such a hodgepodge of different sites to a unified look and feel, you may need to go through this design process on each and every tool independently, since they rarely share code or structure.

But don't give up hope. Many vendors are moving to responsive design for the same reasons I outlined in chapter 1. Some are incorporating responsive design libraries, like Twitter's Bootstrap, which allows them to get up and running with a responsive site quickly and easily.[1] For those vendors that haven't moved to a responsive design, you can make small changes that can go a long way. Some vendors give you a lot of flexibility in customizing the interface yourself, but others don't. In this chapter, I'll show you two different vendor interfaces that I redesigned to be responsive (and more user-friendly). One made it fairly easy for me, and another involved drastic measures.

PLANNING TO MAKE A VENDOR SITE RESPONSIVE

Before you make any progress converting a vendor site to a responsive design, you need to know if it's possible to make the kinds of changes you need to make. You need to ask the following:

- Does the vendor have a mobile site that patrons are automatically redirected to on mobile devices?
- Can you customize the CSS or HTML of the site? Can you customize everything on the site or just the template that surrounds the content the vendor loads?
- Can you add JavaScript to the page? Is the vendor using any frameworks, like jQuery, that you can take advantage of?

These questions will help you understand the scope of what's possible to change on your vendor site. For instance, if patrons on mobile devices are redirected to a mobile site, people on mobile devices won't see your work. They'll get the mobile site instead.

If you can't customize the CSS, but you can customize the HTML, then you can always load your own CSS page after the vendor's CSS with the `<link>` element and override its styles. Of course, the patron will be downloading double the CSS, but the improvements you give them might make it worthwhile.

Next, if you can't customize the HTML or the CSS, sometimes you can add some JavaScript that can do the heavy lifting for you. For instance, Serials Solutions Summon 1.0 doesn't allow libraries to customize the interface of the discovery tool at all, but it does allow libraries to add a custom link to the top navigation. Dave Pattern of the University of Huddersfield was the first to note that you could also include a `<script>` tag in this field and the JavaScript would be parsed. He and I went on to create a number of modifications to Summon, all by leveraging JavaScript to handle inserting the HTML and CSS changes we needed.

The second thing you need to assess is, what, exactly, you need to change:

- How many different layouts does the vendor site have? For instance, our catalog has a different results template depending on whether a patron does a catalog search or a title search.[2] How many different templates will you need to customize?
- How will interaction with the vendor's site change depending on the device size and input type? If the tool relies heavily on text input, how will that affect patrons with touchscreen smartphones? What accommodations to the layout (or interaction) need to be made?
- How will the vendor's content respond on different screen sizes? How will navigation change on smaller screens? On larger screens?

Last, you need to weigh the changes you need to make against what is technically possible. If you really feel that changes to the site's interaction are necessary but you don't have the ability to add JavaScript to the vendor site, then there isn't much you can do. This is also a good time to weigh your own technical abilities against the task you have before you. If you don't have the skills you need to make changes, the library world is full of smart folks who love to share. There's even a good chance that someone else has the same issue with that vendor product and may have already written a fix for it.

TEMPLATES AND PATTERN LIBRARIES

Before you dive in, there is one simple tool you should consider to help simplify your redesign of all of your library sites: a pattern library. A pattern library is simply a set of design patterns that tells you how different parts of your site will look and act, regardless of what system they are in. A pattern library lets you make sure that every time you have a certain element on your site, it looks and behaves the same. It makes it easy to change the look and feel of any system by standardizing the way you write CSS. And while creating a pattern library can take some time up front, you'll save time down the line when you don't have to write new styles for every new site. Pattern libraries give you consistency across the diverse set of vendor tools you work with daily.

Inspired by MailChimp, the innovative e-mail marketing company, I built a pattern library for the GVSU Libraries (figure 9.1).[3] Our pattern library is an interactive HTML document that let's us see how we've solved various design patterns and makes it easy to get the markup and CSS we need to add it to a new project.

As I show you the following examples, refer to my pattern library to understand how I keep our responsive grids, different kinds of navigation lists, and data tables consistent across sites.

EXAMPLE
Atlas Systems' Illiad Interlibrary Loan System and Ares Course Reserve System

At GVSU, we use both Illiad Interlibrary Loan (ILL) and Ares Course Reserve software from Atlas Systems, which makes it easy for students and faculty to manage all of their reserves and ILL requests.[4] Both systems offer a wide range of website customization options, mostly through customizable HTML templates, CSS, and special tokens that are parsed to insert data from a database. The customization

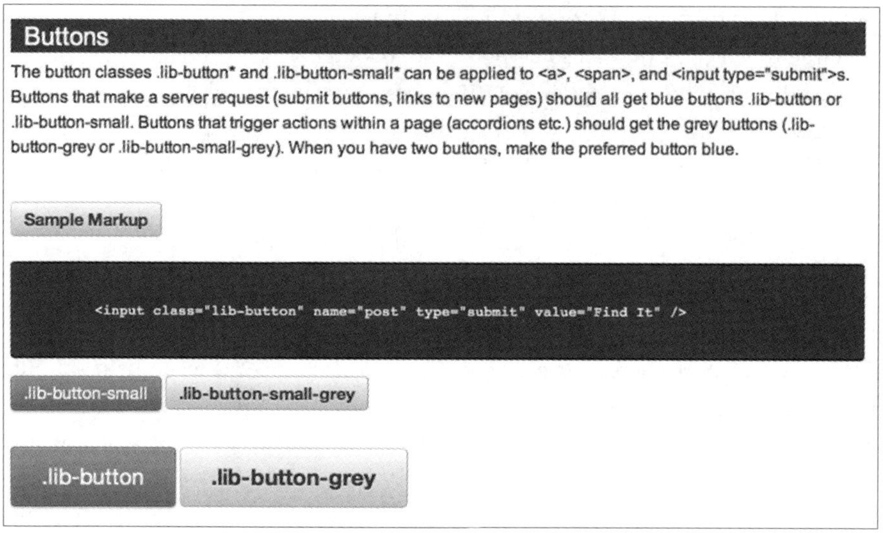

FIGURE 9.1

Our Pattern Library makes it easy to keep a consistent look and feel across all of our services. Here are our buttons.

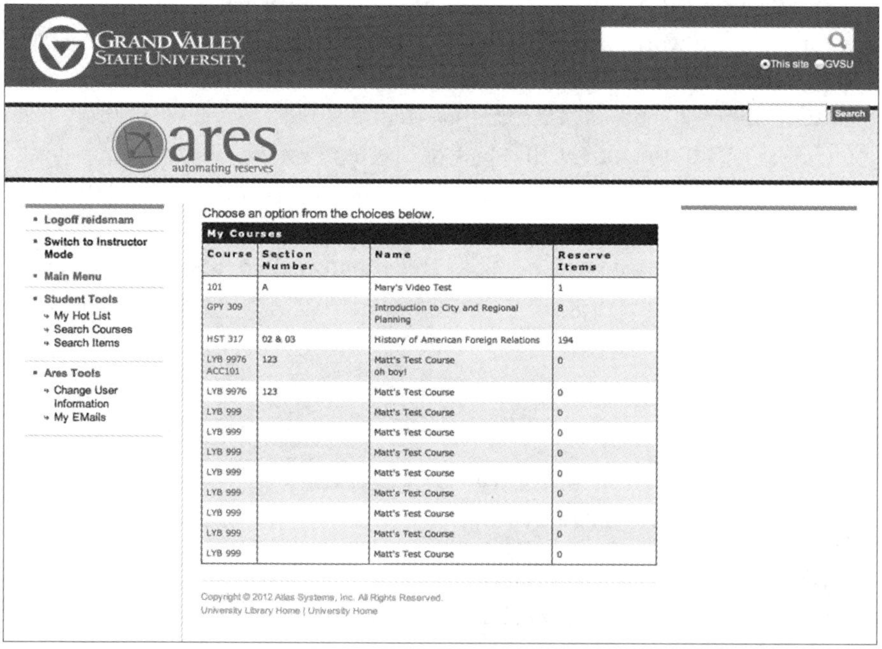

FIGURE 9.2

Ares website wants you to know about Ares.

options are nice, because the default Ares interface leaves a bit to be desired (figure 9.2) (Illiad isn't much better).

One of the first requirements I had (besides removing the Atlas branding) was to make sure the sites were responsive. Despite hearing countless times that no one would *ever* use ILL or course reserves on their phone, I reminded folks that responsive design isn't just about different devices, it's about making sure that we're providing access to anyone and everyone who needs to use the service.[5]

With the easily customizable HTML templates, I was able to transform the default sites into our existing library site template in an afternoon (figure 9.3). But both Ares and Illiad by default display most of their data in tables, which don't always resize nicely for smaller viewports.

In the default version of Illiad, even the forms were wrapped in a table. But thankfully, even though select lists were generated by Illiad tokens, the rest of the form was just straightforward HTML. So I did some analysis of average sizes of entries to see how wide the input fields should be and talked with a few patrons about how they filled out the forms.[6] I was then able to build a more compact form

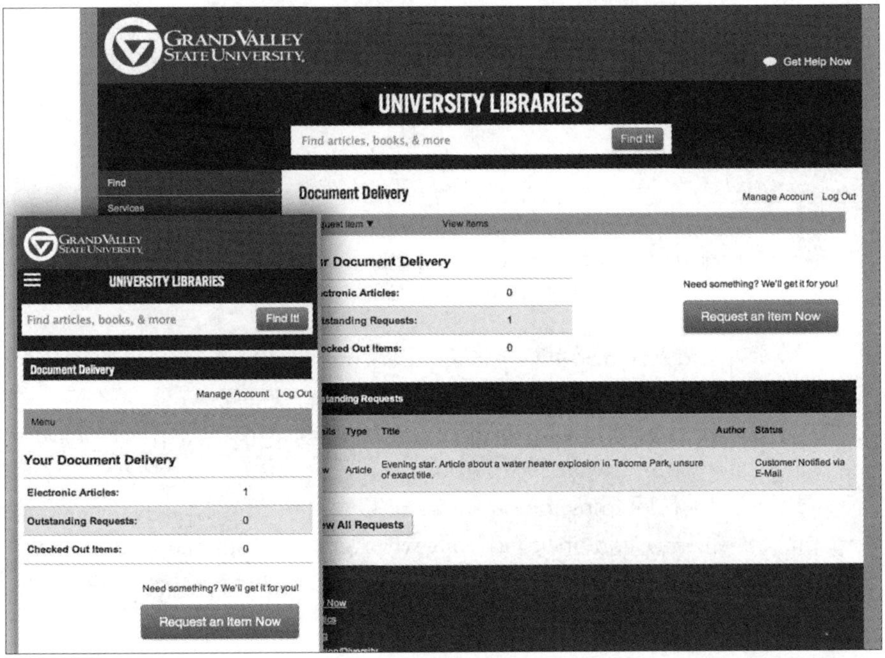

FIGURE 9.3
Illiad is quickly looking like the rest of our library website.

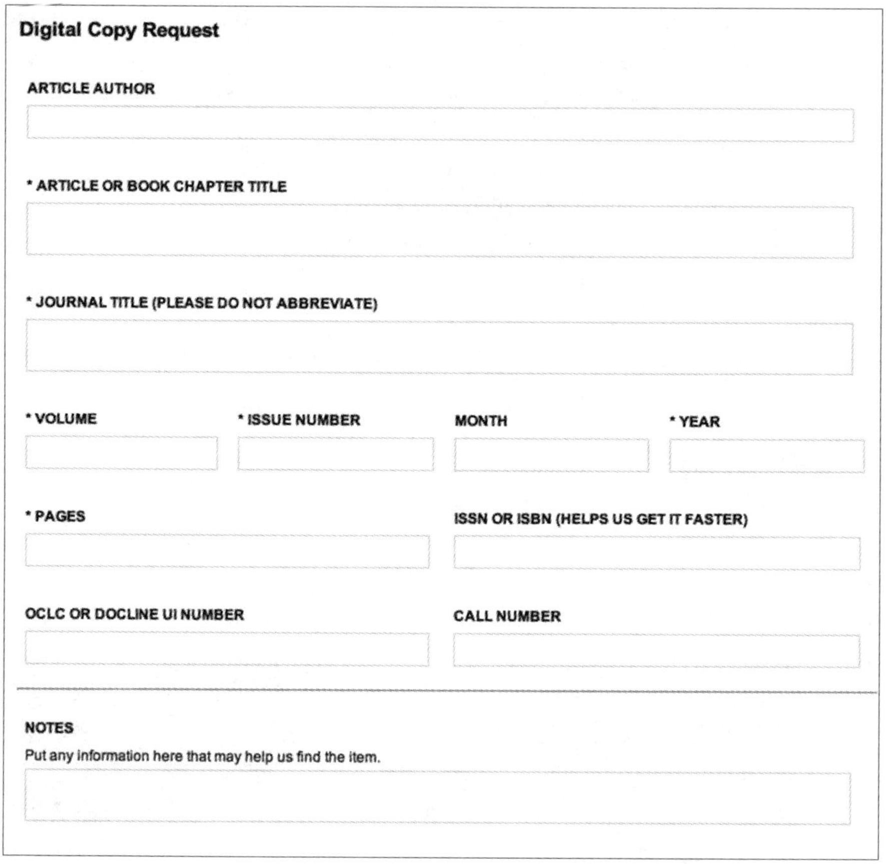
Digital Copy Request

ARTICLE AUTHOR

* ARTICLE OR BOOK CHAPTER TITLE

* JOURNAL TITLE (PLEASE DO NOT ABBREVIATE)

* VOLUME | * ISSUE NUMBER | MONTH | * YEAR

* PAGES | ISSN OR ISBN (HELPS US GET IT FASTER)

OCLC OR DOCLINE UI NUMBER | CALL NUMBER

NOTES

Put any information here that may help us find the item.

FIGURE 9.4
Our form was designed to walk patrons through the request, rather than overwhelm them with fields.

using our CSS grid system, which walked users through the requests in the order they expected the data to appear (figure 9.4).

The grid for the request is built on nested `<div>`s with a few classes applied: one to indicate width (`.span1`) for 100 percent, or one column; (`.span4`) for 25 percent, or four columns, one to indicate float direction on larger viewports (`.right or .left`), and one to indicate whether it has content or not (`.unit`). The (simplified) markup for the form might help illustrate how this works:

```
<div class="line">
    <div class="span1 unit"><!— No float needed —>
        <label>Article Author</label>
        <input name="author" type="text" />
    </div>
</div><!— End .line —>
...
<div class="line">
    <div class="span4 unit left">
        <label>Volume</label>
        <input name="volume" type="text" />
    </div>
    <div class="span4 unit left">
        <label>Issue Number</label>
        <input name="issue" type="text" />
    </div>
    <div class="span4 unit left">
        <label>Month</label>
        <input name="month" type="text" />
    </div>
    <div class="span4 unit left">
        <label>Year</label>
        <input name="year" type="text" />
    </div>
</div><!— End .line —>
<div class="line">
    <div class="span2 unit left">
        <label>Pages</label>
        <input name="pages" type="text" />
    </div>
    <div class="span2 unit left">
        <label>ISSN or ISBN (Helps us get it faster)</label>
        <input name="isbn" type="text" />
    </div>
</div><!— End .line —>
```


The benefit of building this flexible grid is that I use the same classes on all my projects, so creating a grid is second nature to me. And because I built the grid to respond to viewport size, I can predict how each content column will behave. For instance, I know that the `.span4` columns, which on large viewports take up 25

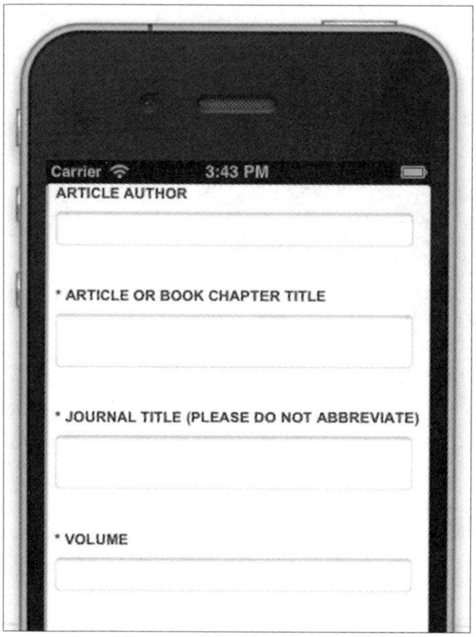

FIGURE 9.5
The Illiad form on a small viewport is still easy-to-use.

percent of their parent element, will spread across 50 percent of the space on viewports around 600 pixels. And on small viewports like phones, no matter which column designation I've used, each column will fill the width of the viewport (figure 9.5).

But forms were only half of it. Much of the data we had to display to our patrons were locked up in clunky, downright inflexible `<table>`s. In Ares, one of the most important tables was the search results when searching by course. While Ares allows us to load GVSU registration data, linking student accounts with the classes they are enrolled in, we haven't worked through all of the political channels to make that happen.[7] And so, at the beginning of each semester, students have to manually add each of their courses.

Once a new semester got under way, we started getting support requests from students who were adding their courses on phones and smaller tablets. They complained that they couldn't find their course among the list, because the tables weren't showing professors' full names. And so a popular course might have ten different sections but no way to distinguish one from the other, since they all had the same course code and title. When I pulled up the site on my phone, I saw what they meant instantly. In our testing, the courses we used all had short titles. But in the wild, course names can be extremely long, and those courses were pushing the final cell of the table off the right side of the screen, cropping the names or, in some cases, making them invisible (figure 9.6).

Even though the table was sized with percentage-based widths, one long word in the class title would force it to be wider than its container. If I were designing this system from scratch, I would have written the markup as a list and not a table, and that alone would probably have prevented this issue. But the table is generated by Ares, and so I would have to reach into my bag of CSS tricks to get the table to display better on the small screen.[8]

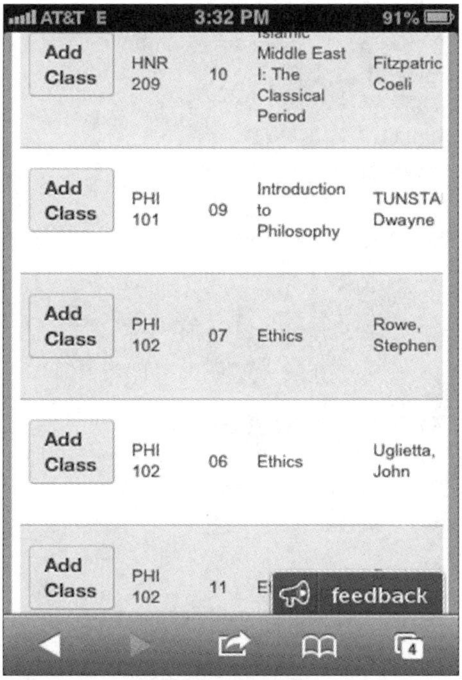

FIGURE 9.6
Professor names were getting cut off on small screens because class titles can be long.

In playing with the longest class titles, I discovered that the problem usually appeared when the viewport was around 410 pixels wide. So to make sure I caught any future long-winded course names, I decided to write my new styles to target viewports smaller than 500 pixels (41.66666666666667 ems, since 1 em = 12 pixels on our site).

First, in my original design, when a course was already added, it would have a button that looked just like the “Add Class” button, but would say “Added.” That made it difficult to distinguish between classes you had already added and ones that might be the class you were looking for. So I replaced the “Added” button with a simple green checkmark, to help distinguish the two types of classes.

After that, I borrowed an idea from Brad Czerniak.[9] Brad's idea was to crunch all of the table cells together, and distinguish the different cells by color. The color serves to help the user know which column the original data belonged to in ab-sence of a table header. But since I wasn't dealing with typical tabular data, and each of the cells contained enough contextual information about its role, I didn't need to bother with the color labels; I just let the content define its own role. Here's a sample of the markup and the new media query:

```
<div class="lib-table">
    <table>
        <tr>
            <td><a class="lib-button-small-grey"  »
              href="#"> Add Class</a></td>
            <td>HNR 209</td><!— Course Number —>
            <td>10</td><!— Section Number —>
```

```
            <td>Islamic Middle East I: The Classical »
              Period</td>
            <td>Professor, Joe</td>
        </tr>
        <tr>
            <td><img src="checkmark.png" alt="Added" /></td>
            <td>PHI 102</td><!— Course Number —>
            <td>3</td><!— Section Number —>
            <td>Ethics</td>
          <td>Professor, Sally</td>
        </tr>
...
/* CSS For this markup */
@media screen and (max-width: 41.66666666666667em){
    .lib-table table {
        display:block;
    }
    .lib-table table td {
        background: #fff;
        border: 0;
        display: inline;
        float: left;
        padding: 0 0 0 .25em;
        /* Add space before each cell */
        width:auto;
    }
    .lib-table table thead th {
        display: none; /* Don't show the table headers */
    }
    .lib-table table td:after {
        /* Add a comma after each item */
        content: ',';
    }
    .lib-table table td:first-child:after,
    .lib-table table td:last-child:after {
        /* But no comma after first or last item */
        content: '';
    }
}
```


The result is a nice display on small screens of each class name, it's course number, the professor, and whether you've already added it (figure 9.7). And best

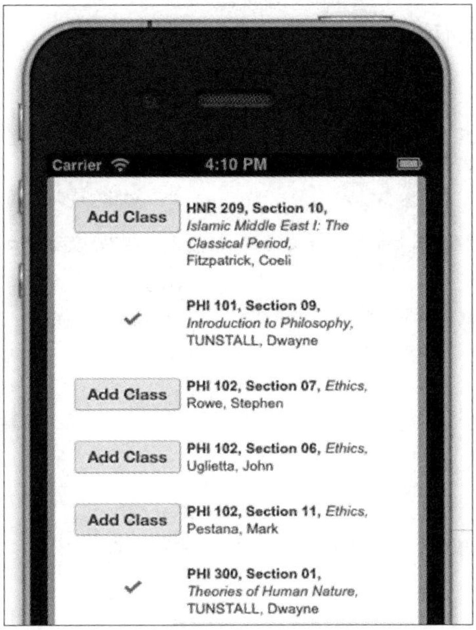

FIGURE 9.7
The Revised search results table on small screens, with a wicked CSS hack.

of all, it shows all the data, never letting professor names disappear off the side of the screen.

We've done a lot of work to customize not only the look and feel of Illiad and Ares but also how patrons interact with them. If you want to see more, you can take a look at our code on GitHub: http://github.com/gvsulib.

RADICAL MEASURES EXAMPLE
Serials Solutions 360Link Link Resolver

While CSS can often help make vendor-supplied tables responsive, often you need to make more drastic changes to the vendor site's layout to improve usability. We ran into this issue with our Serials Solutions 360Link link resolver.[10] While Serials Solutions would work with us to change the markup of our link resolver, we wanted to make the changes continuously as we analyzed usage and ran usability

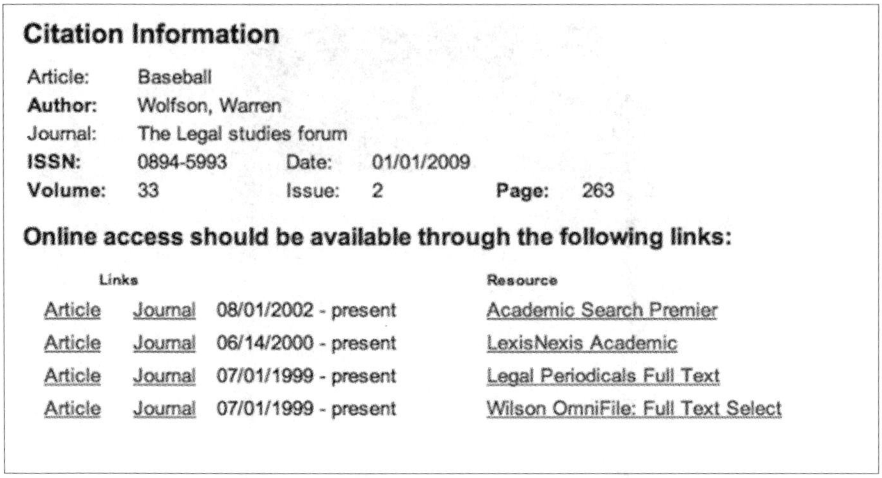

FIGURE 9.8
By default, the link resolver creates a link matrix that confuses users.

tests. So we decided to take radical measures to make our link resolver responsive and more usable.

When patrons get to the link resolver from our discovery system or an abstracting and indexing database, they are presented with a clunky, table-based citation and a big matrix of links to the full text of the article, the journal the article appears in, and the database the journal is available in (figure 9.8).

Since the goal of the link resolver is to connect the patron with the item they are looking for, the goal of this page should have been to make it as obvious as possible where to click to find the article. But it wasn't. Many of our users would click on the database or journal links rather than the "Article" link, because we've trained them to look for terms like "Full Text" rather than "Article." And because the table was full on inline styles, it was close to impossible to use on small viewports.

The first step was to use CSS to style the table-based list to be as usable as possible. Because the "Article" links are the most important, we styled them to be blue buttons and styled the "Journal" links as light gray buttons. Since the database link isn't really useful if the "Journal" and "Article" links fail, we didn't want folks using it, so we styled it to look like it wasn't a link. Testing showed an immediate understanding on the part of our patrons about the hierarchy of these links, and folks were much more likely to click "Article" than before (figure 9.9). But now our patrons were confused about *which* article link to click, since there wasn't anything cluing them in to the hierarchy of rows.

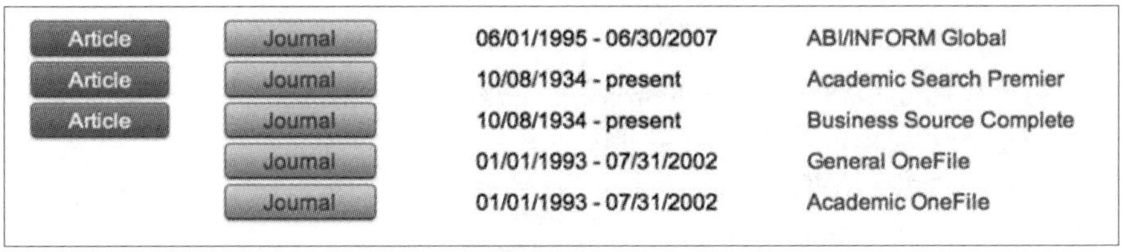

FIGURE 9.9
It's more obvious which link to click with a little CSS.

We rank our databases on the basis of how likely our patrons are to actually find the full text they've been promised, so in general, we want the patron to click the first link. We had some ideas for how to communicate that, but they were all difficult with the table-based structure full of duplicated IDs and inconsistently applied classes in the default 360Link markup. In addition, the `<table>` kept the page from playing nicely with small viewports. So we decided to take the next step and fix the markup in the browser, with JavaScript.

First, we needed to capture the data we needed from the page so we could use them in our new markup. Since we were already using jQuery, this was simple. I wrote a simple loop that iterated over each row of the results table and captured the links and other data into JavaScript variables:

```
var articleLinks = new Array(); var journalLinks = new
  Array(); var results;
$(“table#JournalLinkTable”).find(“tr”).each(function(index)
{
    // For each tr in the table with the id
    // of JournalLinkTable, run this function.
    if($(this).find(“#ArticleCL a”).length > 0) {
        // Look for an article link. If there is one,
        // save its href in the articleLinks array
        // at the index point
        articleLinks[index] = $(this).find(“#ArticleCL a”).
attr(“href”);
} else {
        // No article link. Note that in the articleLink
        // array
        articleLinks[index] = “NA”;
    }
    // Do this with the Journal link, the database name
    // and link, and the date range, using the
```

```
    // appropriate variables.
...
    // Get the total number of results in the results
    // variable
    results = index;
});
```

After running this function, I now have a set of JavaScript arrays with all of the data from the confusing results table. In the example from figure 9.9, my database Names array looks like this:

```
databaseNames = (
    "AB/INFORM Global",
    "Academic Search Premier",
    "Business Source Complete",
    "General OneFile",
    "Academic OneFile"
);
```


All that's left is to replace the old table markup with something a bit more semantic and flexible, using all of the data I saved from the old table as content. In this example, I'm assuming that the `<table id="JournalLinksTable">` is wrapped in a `<div>` with an ID of `LinkResults`. I just need to create some new markup using this data. I'll create a loop that runs over each item in each of my arrays and generates new HTML from the content (line breaks added for readability and date ranges and journal links left out for simplicity):[11]

```
var content = '<ul class="results">';
for (var i = 0; i < articleLinks.length; i++) {
    // Is there a link to the Full Text?
    // If not, link to Journal
    var hRef = (articleLinks[i] != 'NA') ? articleLinks[i] »
       : journalLinks[i];
    var label = (articleLinks[i] != 'NA') ? "Full Text »
      Online" : "Browse Journal";
    content = content + '
        <li>
            <a href="' + hRef + '" class="articleLink"> »
              ' + label + '
            </a> from
```

```
                <a href="' + databaseLinks[i] + '" »
                  class="database"> ' + databaseNames[i] + '
                </a>
            </li>
content = content + '</ul>';
// Now replace the old content with the new
$("#LinkResults").html(content);
```

At the end of this process, I'll have all of my content in a semantic `<ul>` that I can style as I wish. This lets me have more flexibility with layout on small viewports, but it also lets me change the way patrons interact with the results set. I'll add just a little CSS to get the list looking more like it's tabled self:

```
.articleLink {
     font-size: 1.125em;
     font-weight: bold;
     text-decoration: none;
}
.databaseLink {
     color: #333;
     font-weight: bold;
     text-decoration: none;
}
/*  Make the first result bigger,
and style the full-text link like a button */
ul.results li:first-child {
     font-size: 1.375em;
}
ul.results li:first-child a.articleLink {
     background: #0090D2;
     border: 1px solid #4081AF;
     border-bottom-color: #20559A;
     border-radius: 4px;
     color: #fff !important;
     display: inline-block;
     margin: 0 0 .5em 0;
     padding:  .227em 0.6818em;
     text-align: center;
}
ul.results li:first-child a.databaseLink {
     font-weight: normal;
}
```

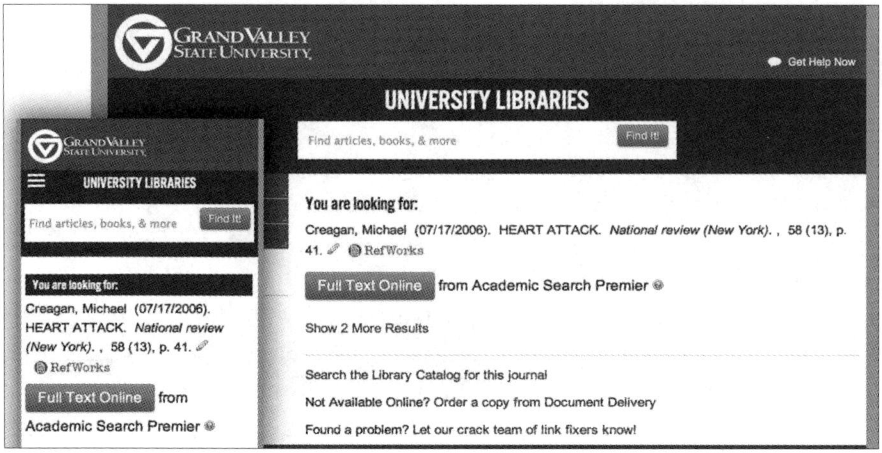

FIGURE 9.10
Our new link resolver looks great on any device, and is easy to use.

This simplified list now shows the first link prominently and lists alternative sources for the content below. But best of all, it looks great on any size viewport, since the tables have been replaced by more flexible markup (figure 9.10).[12]

In our live version, we hide all but the first result with jQuery and then give our patrons the option "Show More Results." Patrons without JavaScript or where JavaScript fails get a nicely styled matrix of links (as seen in figure 9.9). But patrons with JavaScript get an enhanced version of the tool that makes it even easier to get to the article or book chapter they need.

Armed with this new understanding of fluid grids, flexible media, CSS media queries, and the basics of site performance, we're ready to tackle any aspect of the library website, from the home page to hosted vendor systems. And by designing great experiences for every viewport, we'll step off the treadmill of designing for the next hot device. Your patrons will thank you, no matter how they visit your library website.

NOTES

1. Bootstrap, http://getbootstrap.com.
2. This completely boggles my mind.
3. MailChimp's original pattern library can be seen at the Flickr page of aarronwalter, www.flickr.com/photos/aarronwalter/5579386649/sizes/l/; the GVSU Libraries Pattern Library is online at www.gvsu.edu/library/ui.

4. More information on these systems is at the website of Atlas Systems, www.atlas-sys.com. Illiad is now owned or maintained by OCLC, but the software still betrays its foundation as an Atlas project.
5. I'd like to also point out that 40 percent of our support requests in the first six months after the redesign on both systems came from folks on phones. So *there*.
6. Most actually never filled out the forms, since they use OpenURL requests from Abstract databases or our link resolver. When I was a kid, we had to fill out our ILL requests manually.
7. Ahem.
8. There is a great roundup of solutions to responsive tables by Chris Coyers at http://css-tricks.com/responsive-data-table-roundup/.
9. Brad Czerniak. *Another Responsive Data Tables Approach*. https://web.archive.org/web/20130530142004/http://hawidu.com/2011/04/27/another-responsive-data-tables-approach/.
10. A link resolver is a piece of software that helps connect references to things like articles in one electronic resource to the full text of that article in an academic journal.
11. The more sophisticated version of this function also parses out whether the item is available online or in print, as well as providing a tool tip that shows date coverage and provides journal access.
12. The source code for our link resolver script is available at https://github.com/gvsulib/360Link-Reset.

Index